I0022524

PLÁTICAS

PLÁTICAS

Conversations
About and Among
Friends and
Neighbors
in Cuba,
New Mexico

Esther V. Cordova May

SUNSTONE
PRESS

SANTA FE

All photographs not otherwise attributed
are from the author's personal collection.

© 2018 by Esther V. Cordova May
All Rights Reserved.

No part of this book may be reproduced in any form or by any electronic or mechanical means including
information storage and retrieval systems without permission in writing from the publisher,
except by a reviewer who may quote brief passages in a review.

Sunstone books may be purchased for educational, business, or sales promotional use.
For information please write: Special Markets Department, Sunstone Press,
P.O. Box 2321, Santa Fe, New Mexico 87504-2321.

Book and cover design › Vicki Ahl
Body typeface › Book Antiqua
∞
Printed on acid-free paper

Library of Congress Cataloging-in-Publication Data

Names: May, Esther V. Cordova, 1936- author.
Title: Pláticas : conversations about and among friends and neighbors in
   Cuba, New Mexico / by Esther V. Cordova May.
Other titles: Conversations about and among friends and neighbors in Cuba,
   New Mexico
Description: Santa Fe, NM : Sunstone Press, [2018] | Includes bibliographical
   references and index.
Identifiers: LCCN 2017053161 | ISBN 9781632932099 (softcover : alk. paper)
Subjects: LCSH: Cuba (N.M.)--History--Anecdotes. | Cuba (N.M.)--Folklore. |
   Country life--New Mexico--Cuba--History--Anecdotes. | City and town
   life--New Mexico--Cuba--History--Anecdotes. | Community life--New
   Mexico--Cuba--History--Anecdotes. | Cuba (N.M.)--Social life and
   customs--Anecdotes. | Folklore--New Mexico--Cuba. | Cuba
   (N.M.)--Biography--Anecdotes.
Classification: LCC F804.C95 M395 2018 | DDC 978.9/57--dc23
LC record available at https://lccn.loc.gov/2017053161

THE PAPER USED IN THIS BOOK IS FROM RESPONSIBLY MANAGED FORESTS.

WWW.SUNSTONEPRESS.COM
SUNSTONE PRESS / POST OFFICE BOX 2321 / SANTA FE, NM 87504-2321 /USA
(505) 988-4418 / ORDERS ONLY (800) 243-5644 / FAX (505) 988 1025

CONTENTS

PART I

Pláticas de la Gente de Cuba, Nuevo Mexico   13
(Conversations, People, Places and Things
Related to Cuba New Mexico)

Part II

Pláticas de Tristezas y Amor   99
(Conversations about Sadness and Love)

Part III

Pláticas Formal Presentadadas a Audiencias   127
(Formal Presentations to an Audience)

PREFACE

I knew from the start that *Pláticas: Conversations About and Among Friends and Neighbors in Cuba, New Mexico* was going to be a different kind of book than *Antes: Stories from the Past: Rural Cuba, New Mexico, 1769–1949*. As in *Antes*, the history is solid. It is in the basic configuration of the text that is different as is the emphasis on content. In many instances, the structure and form of the writing also differs from Antes.

Pláticas, for those of us who still pursue this archaic form of dialogue, know there is no set formula for our dialogue as are reflected in parts of this book or in a real conversation. Having decided that *pláticas* were what I wanted to write about, share with my community and relate to those beyond, I used that format for this book.

I learned from many years of reading Native American author Leslie Marmon Silko from Laguna Pueblo that as non-traditional writers, we can direct our style of writing to reflect our cultural traits. These reflections can include writing in the style that we think, speak and respond to events in our lives and the lives of those we write about. In many instances, such as in the chapter titled "Conversations about Sadness and Love," differ from those of mainstream society. Yet, among friends, neighbors and cousins, it is acceptable to recount our pain as well as our love.

It is also culturally appropriate to give recognition where recognition is due, for instance, in the marvelous efforts of Fidencio and Julia Aragon in their building of their replica of Cuba's 1915 church. This was truly a labor of love, as the title indicates.

We don't all think alike, look alike or wish or pray toward the same ends. Fortunately, there is room and time for all of us to appreciate what each of us can bring to the art of sincere conversation.

ACKNOWLEDGEMENTS

It is certain that without many hours of help from my husband and best friend, Don Moore, my major source of technical help, this book would never have been completed. Although Don jokingly claims he "only works for food," his help has been constant. (I do feed him regularly also!) In truth, it has been his sharp technical skills and willingness to retype and edit every single change in manuscripts that has given us the finished project called *Pláticas*.

My heartfelt thanks to dear friends Judy Gutierrez Casaus and her one-hundred-four-year-old aunt, Sadie Ochoa, who wants to see this book come to fruition. Their continuous encouragement is deeply appreciated. "Aunt Sadie" and my mother were best friends in school and young adulthood and I want her to share in the completion of this book.

I will be forever grateful to my cousin Frances Salaz Oliva who so generously shared her knowledge of our grandmother Leonor's legacy. Her gift of materials and photographs opened a whole new dimension to our shared heritage.

My dear cousin, Frances Santillanes, who is always willing to listen to me relate my latest computer disaster or complaints about how tired I am deserves special recognition for her undying loyalty and her encouragement to proceed with my writing. Then there are my cousins Robert (Bert) Sanchez and Benito DeLaO Valdez, who pray a lot on behalf of my getting this book to see the light of day.

I extend my special thanks also to my bookish friends, Lee and Ross Smith, Danny Gallardo, Terri Otto and Sara D'Alessandro who are forever finding books which are inspiring and usually marvelously helpful. Also, I offer Jean Anderson my sincere gratitude for thirty-five years of friendship and unending, enriching conversation.

I do not know whether my friends at the Sandoval County Historical Society pray on my behalf but they are always there to support me in every way they can. Thank you, Martha Liebert, Roy Skeen, Rusty and Dirk Van Hart, Max C de Baca, Connie Aguilar and Lorraine Dominguez. Most special thanks to my dear "Rio Puerco brother," Nasario Garcia who is such a source of inspiration and *hermandad* (brotherhood, affinity).

Thanks also to all of you who so willingly gave your consent to print your family members' names as part of this work. Having your consent has given me the freedom to share what I have felt in my heart about your loved ones. Despite the many unforetold obstacles, together we have our *Pláticas* in book form. We also have our history, our language and our identity.

Again, thanks to the *Cuba News* staff, Peggy Ohler and Carolyn Melgard, for publishing the original *Pláticas* articles between September 2013 and August, 2014. Your support and loyalty have been a source of professional encouragement to me since my first articles appeared in the *Cuba News* in November, 2007. To all of the wonderful people who wished me well when I set you and me on this challenging journey back in 2013, I thank you for your trust in me. For your sake, I wish I had given you more. Finally, to all the staff at Sunstone Press, thank you again for answering my many questions and for your support.

At all times, it has been my aim to give recognition to as many people who have contributed so unselfishly of their resources so that this place we call home will be a place we recall with love and affection. (Please send no "tweets." I only accept tweets from the magpies outside my door.)

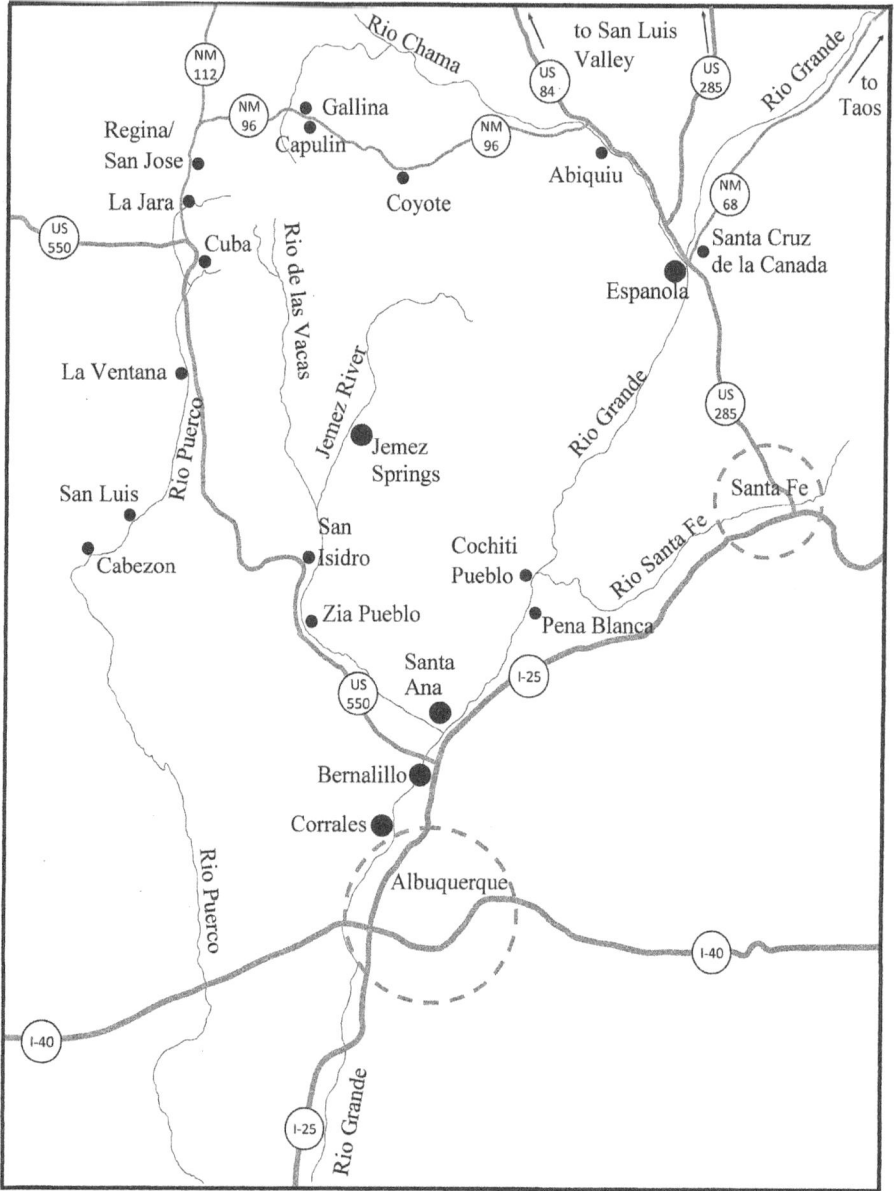

Map of the Region

INTRODUCTION

Many years ago, my dear friend, Jean Anderson, introduced me to the works of the late author and poet May Sarton. At the time, I recall finding Ms. Sarton's work slightly too homey, rather personal, yet interestingly inspiring and informative enough to keep a reader's attention. Several years later, I came across yet another book of May Sarton's poetry titled: *Coming Into Eighty*. At that time, I was younger and not very interested in reading poetry related to becoming as old as eighty. Now, I too am eighty years old and I feel an urgency to relate *las pláticas de mis vecinos*, (the conversations among my Cuba, New Mexico neighbors and friends), before all memory of these treasures is lost.

There is also the creative urge to share my own role and my perspective related to specific events as a participating member of the community of Cuba. These would include some of the lectures and presentations I have delivered over the years that I have enjoyed as a resident of the place of my birth and where my own history has been enriched. In addition, there are the elegies and eulogies honoring, in most cases, the untimely deaths of former students, friends and family members.

I have always done a lot of journal writing, which in many instances was expressed poetically. At this time, I feel confident enough to share some of it with my readers.

The poetry included is free form and in many cases bilingual or in Spanish. These too are derived from *pláticas*, some of which occurred in my dreams. Others transpired during periods of deep sorrow. Of these, it can be said some arose out of conversations with my innermost self. Conversations none the less.

It is my hope that, like May Sarton, at this stage in my life I will still be able to inspire my readers and interest them in the now nearly lost art of conversation. Some have said that conversation is one of the most intimate contacts between individuals. A one-hundred-forty-character message on an electronic device does not take the place of a conversation. A conversation is an exchange of information and ideas. Ideas, if they are to be shared, require thinking, as well as acute listening. Among family and neighbors, *pláticas* have the potential of being meaningful, sincere, empathetic and, in many cases, reassuring and comforting.

It is my hope that the *pláticas* in this book meet these criteria in written form and that the result will allow a return to real dialogue about the serious issue that beset us today. A further goal that I hope can be accomplished through our consequential dialogue are empathy for those among us who may be different from ourselves. The measure of the future on our environment and our society will be determined by how sincere and empathetically we are in our conversations.

Cuba is no longer the world of *Antes* (our past). Cuba is a twenty-first century, dying town. The success of the generations that follow will need competence at expressing their needs and describing the skill set they possess in order to survive. For these tasks, they will need to know how to communicate in their dominant language as well as a second and perhaps a third language. I know from experience that those among us who have remained bilingual or multilingual, already have an advantage over our monolingual counterparts.

As an eighty-year-old member of this community that I love, I hope that there are still enough of us left who can sincerely say to a friend or neighbor, without the aid of an iPhone, *"Buenos dias. ¿Como estás?"* (Good morning. How are you?)

Most of the *pláticas* are stories held in common, stories and events remembered by many or perhaps just a few of us who shared a specific time in this place we call home.

As I approached eighty years of age, like May Sarton, I am comfortable in this stage of my life and once again look forward to continuing the discourses we call *pláticas*.

PART I

Pláticas de la Gente de Cuba, Nuevo Mexico
(Conversations, People, Places
and Things Related to
Cuba New Mexico)

Una Plática Sobre La Curanderia
(A Conversation About Folk Healing)

Traditionally in rural New Mexico, *Curanderia* (folk healing arts and practices) has been, in large measure, how we survived in times of sickness and injuries. Our folk healers and practitioners were known as *Curanderas* (female) or *Curanderos* (male). *Medicas* and *Parteras* (both female) were related more to midwifery, or female disorders. In our communities, there was deep cultural acceptance as well as respect for these people's roles and for the remedies they used.

Since around February 2013, when the very popular film *Bless Me Última* was released, talk pertaining to folk healing and its relationship to witchcraft began to arise in conversations. These conversations were probably due to the impressions gleaned from the actions of the main character, *Última*, the folk healer. The film is based on the book by the same title, written by New Mexico author, Rodolfo Anaya. It is my perception that upon seeing the film some people came away thinking that folk healing is a form of quackery related to witchcraft and sorcery. In Spanish, such acts are called *brujeria* (witchcraft). These are the practices of a person believed to be a witch. Although many people here in Cuba did not believe in witchcraft there were some who did. As seen in the film, the owl was looked upon as Última's alter ego. Locally, owls were looked upon as bad omens. In olden times, many an owl was shot down for being seen dangerously close to someone's house in the belief that someone wanted to put a curse upon a member of the family. There was also a very popular expression that said *pongo te las cruces* used in conjunction with the sign of the cross. This would be directed at an individual relating some outrageous or unbelievable story or event and that by making the sign of the cross the listener would ward off the evil spirit associated with the event or prevent a curse from occurring. Because there were people who believed in witchcraft or were superstitious, our local *curanderas* were frequently called upon to take care of a baby or small child believed to have had *el mal de ojo* (the evil eye) cast upon them. This *maleficio* (bewitching or being made ill through witchcraft) was usually attributed to an overly enthusiastic admirer or perhaps a jealous relative or friend. This was especially true if the baby was considered to be particularly beautiful or charming among the adult members of the family.

There were also people who truly believed they were subject to *maleficios* by strangers. These people wore garlic cloves around their necks in order to avoid becoming sick from the evils of witchcraft. In Lesley Gordon's *A Country Herbal,* among the many uses for garlic she says, "it was believed to have magic properties and was carried as a talisman in China, Japan, Greece and Turkey." She also says that German miners took it with them into mines as a charm against evil spirits." Basically, these were the same reasons people here wore the garlic cloves around their necks or pinned to their clothing. Garlic is also supposed to be strongly aphrodisiac. Given the strong and lasting smell of garlic, I would have to agree with Ms. Gordon who says, it should be used for this purpose "only between consenting garlic eaters."

There was also a disorder called *melarchico-ca*, which translates to depressed; homesick; listless; melancholy or sad. When babies became subject to this disorder people believed that a red ribbon tied on their wrist would cure the melancholy. Similarly, soon after a baby was born pieces of the reddest coral beads were pinned to the baby's clothing or tied to his or her wrist. As an inquisitive youngster, I once asked why that was done to one of my newborn cousins. My great-aunt firmly informed me the coral beads were to ward off bad things happening to the baby. Since then, I always assumed the coral was more a good luck charm when in fact the coral, like the red ribbon, was probably used to prevent the child from becoming *melarchico*.

Among the more common ailments our local *curanderas* were called upon to attend to were people in distress with something called *empache* (severe indigestion). *Empache* was not related to a *maleficio* or bewitching. This was a common disorder that likely followed an event where a person had overindulged in eating too much. For instance, children (and some adults as well) were frequently warned not to eat too much freshly baked bread that had not cooled yet, lest they would become *empachado*. Other such foods we were warned about were *posole* and *carne adovada,* both rich in pork. If one became a victim of *empache* it was a major case of indigestion. As a verb, *empachar,* the dictionaries translate this condition as surfeit, meaning overindulgence, especially in food or drink. Apparently among the discomforts associated with *empache* were confusion and perplexity. These symptoms seem to match the old television commercial, "I can't believe I ate the whole thing." Not believing what one has done at a feast where much good food and drink was available could be very bewildering and painful indeed. The *curandera* would be summoned to the patient's home and the remedies for this ailment would be prepared and administered until the patient recovered. The remedies for this condition could vary widely from simple teas made from cinnamon, or chamomile to something more potent such as juniper berries. Naturally, this would depend on the severity of the patient's condition at the time the *curandera* intervened.

It is understandable how someone not familiar with the folk culture of northern New Mexico could simply dismiss the whole notion of this tradition. For example, in *VOX: New College Spanish/English Dictionary,* it says a *curandero,* is a quack doctor. On the other hand, Ruben Cobos' *Dictionary of New Mexico and Southern Colorado Spanish,* says a *curandero* is a folk healer. Cobos also states that a *medica* is a term applied to a female folk healer who is a midwife as well. Cobos defines a *partera* as a midwife. Also, very common among the folk healing practitioners in northern New Mexico were the *sobadores*. Cobos defines them as persons who set dislocated bones, or gave someone a rub down or massage. Interestingly when it comes to defining the term *bruja,* which most people instantly refer to this person as a witch, Cobos adds: "psychic" a person with" extrasensory perception". In defining the male *brujo* instead of female witch, Cobos says, "sorcerer; Indian medicine man;"

These different sources leave a mixed impression of who our folk healers might have been. However, the official source of our mother tongue, *Diccionario De La Lengua Española Real Academia Espanola,* says a *curandero,* male or female, is a person dedicated to the practice of healing without benefit of an official title or degree. Culturally and traditionally, this is what these people were in the rural hamlets of northern New Mexico. We depended on the "extrasensory perception" of these gifted people rather than an official degree or certification. As well, we learned from them and our native neighbors which herbal remedies would make us feel better or heal our wounds.

Michael Moore, in his book *Los Remedies Traditional: Herbal Remedies of the Southwest,* says of our sources of folk remedies, "The early Spanish settlers brought their traditional herbs, such as *manzanilla* (chamomile) and *alhucema* (lavender); the Pueblo Indians introduced them to *inmortal* (antelope horns) and *osha.* Present usage is the result of nearly five hundred years of Spanish and over a thousand years of Indian pragmatism". In the absences of more advanced medical practices, the folk healers in our region and culture used the resources they had to aid their sick and injured family members and neighbors. Health services in rural northern New Mexico, even following statehood in 1912, were virtually nonexistent. During the period known as our Territorial Era (1848–1912), the political structure and the "movers and shakers" were far more interested in grabbing as much land and resources as possible from our farmers, ranchers and native tribes, than they were in providing appropriate health care. In her book, *Social Housekeeping,* Sandra Schackel quotes what President William Howard Taft told the New Mexico delegation on January 6, 1912, as New Mexico officially became a state. The President is quoted as having said: "Well, it's all over now. I am glad to give you life. I hope you will be healthy". In fact, at the very time New Mexico had finally gained statehood our population was in a terrible health crisis. Our people were suffering and dying from such communicable diseases as diphtheria, typhoid and tuberculosis. During that period, tuberculosis was rampant throughout the population and continued to be a serious health issue until the 1950s when antibiotics became part of the treatment for this debilitating disease. Furthermore, the newly declared 47th State of the United States had the highest infant mortality rate in the nation. Infant mortality rate is a statistic commonly used to determine the general wellbeing and health of an area or a society. Our rural population in New Mexico was obviously not in good health. Our newborn babies and vulnerable young children were dying in large numbers and many more were suffering from lack of basic health care. It is obvious that President Taft had not been well briefed on how severe health conditions were in New Mexico, making his statement totally inappropriate.

There is still another irony related to the 1912 Presidential wishes for good health in New Mexico. By the middle 1800s, long before statehood in 1912, the railroads had become well entrenched in New Mexico and were looking to enhance travel westward. The result was that thousands of easterners known as" health-seekers" were flocking to New Mexico to restore their health. The railroad companies had very successfully advertised New Mexico as having the best climate to restore the health of eastern city dwellers. Many of these newcomers were suffering from "consumption", otherwise known as tuberculosis, which was the leading killer of the nineteenth century. While these health-seekers were relaxing in resorts and sanatoriums enjoying the healing waters of our mineral springs and our hot, dry climate, the few doctors that were available in the state at that time were at their service. Generally, these doctors were providing the health-seekers with modern professional health care while the local rural population remained dependent on our faithful *curanderas* and *parteras* and their knowledge of folk remedies.

It is important and interesting to note that these folk healers in rural New Mexico practiced with a very important skill set which wouldn't be recognized until the 1920s, when the state was trying, in many cases unsuccessfully, to implement health care services in some rural communities. The success of the local folk healers became particularly evident as our *curanderas* and *medicas* treated female patients and young children. These *curanderas,* including Cuba's own Doña Gregorita Sanchez and Doña Victoria Aragon, were members of our community and, like their counterparts in other villages, they spoke the local language. They were well known and trusted by their female patients. Furthermore, there were the delicate issues of modesty as it related to intimate conditions such as sex and reproduction, which were not discussed with strangers. Most importantly, the patient and healer shared a belief in the remedies as well as in the procedures being performed.

When I was about ten years old, I recall Doña Gregorita coming to our house because my mother was very sick and needed her services. I remember her as being a rather small, gentle and soft-spoken woman who moved with precision, almost like a dancer. She wore an immaculately clean apron and her hair was combed back in a traditional bun. She soon began to ask the female members of the family who were present for some of the things she might need following her initial examination of my mother, her patient. A short time after Doña Gregorita had been examining her, she came out of the room where she and my mother had been. She told my father that my mother needed to be gotten to a hospital immediately. In the meantime, the women in the house were instructed on how to best prepare my mother to get to the hospital as safely as possible. My father knew he could not get her to the nearest hospital, ninety miles away, in our pickup truck, the only vehicle we owned. He hurried to town to find a friend or relative with a car willing to take my critically ill mother to an Albuquerque hospital. My father soon came back to tell Doña Gregorita that the car would soon be there. He quickly changed his clothes and when the car and driver arrived, my seriously ailing mother, with help from Doña Gregorita and the other women, was loaded into the sedan and my grandmother and father left with her for the two to three-hour bumpy ride to Albuquerque. Doña Gregorita picked up her things, thanked the women in the house and asked if there was someone there to take her home.

My point in telling this story has to do with the integrity and care the *curanderas* practiced in attending their patients. It is likely that, upon talking to my mother during the examination, Doña Gregorita discovered my mother's case was beyond anything she could handle and told my father what his options were. The truth was my mother was suffering from the affects of an ectopic pregnancy, a pregnancy occurring outside the uterus usually in a fallopian tube. Since pregnancy was one of Doña Gregorita's specialties, she recognized the symptoms, knew her limitations in such complicated cases and referred the patient to the professionals in Albuquerque. In doing so, she saved my mother's life. My mother survived and recovered from the surgical procedure needed and lived to be nine-ty-three years old.

I don't recall Doña Victoria as vividly as I do Doña Gregorita, except that she was tall and slender and I don't recall that she ever came to our house. I would have known her only as a member of our community. I would have also known where she lived and that she was one of our *curanderas* who took care of sick people and delivered babies.

Our *sobadores* too, would go to people's houses. This was especially true if it was suspected that the patient might have a fractured limb. A *sobador*, wanting to reset a dislocated bone or put a splint on a fracture, would not want the patient moved. The alternative was for the *sobador* to go to the patient. Again, the patient was at home, surrounded by family in familiar surroundings. These conditions alone would reduce the level of stress. Barring complications such as infection, these patients would be more likely to heal faster than in an unfamiliar environment among strangers. As well, most local people only spoke Spanish or one of our several indigenous languages until after World War II and most professional health care givers only spoke English.

I recall that shortly before World War II, local merchants started to bring antiseptics such as iodine, mercurochrome and rubbing alcohol for sale. There was also aspirin in tiny metal boxes. As well, we had periodic visits from "the Raleigh man," a door-to-door salesman in a small van with his supply of home products. It was from this source that people bought little cans of cinnamon, cloves, ginger and bottles of vanilla. He also introduced lotions and liniments for skin care. Wonderful as these products were, there were few people who could afford them so most continued to rely on traditional herbs and analgesic bark from willow trees to relieve their aches and pains.

Generally speaking, New Mexico was slow in implementing modern health practices as opposed to the folk healing and caring that was the major source of health care. It was not until the ravages of the 1918–1919 influenza epidemic that people in positions of power and influence were motivated to act on significant measures toward better health care. Locally, people claim the winter of 1917–1918 had the worst death rate ever experienced in Cuba and surrounding areas. Other sources say the influenza epidemic arrived in New Mexico in late 1918. Regardless of the exact time the influenza was detected, the truth was this disease took a tremendous toll among our people. Sources such as Sandra Schackel in her book, *Social Housekeeping*, states that at least 15,000 cases were recorded in the state, resulting in 1,055 reported deaths. This epidemic became obvious evidence that the state had neither the structure nor the machinery to cope with an emergency of this magnitude.

I have been told of households that lost as many as ten members of their immediate and extended families during this catastrophic event. These casualties consisted primarily of young, usually pregnant women vulnerable children and the elderly. Such losses resulted in villages such as Cuba with a generation of orphaned children. These children were then left in the care of sometimes reluctant maiden aunts, stepmothers or grandparents with few resources or abilities to care for another child. Some of these orphaned children never got over the indignities and painful experiences they suffered following the deaths of their mothers. My own father and his two younger sisters experienced such circumstances after the death of their mother in 1918.

These children's fathers, in many instances, were away for long periods of time working in the sheep camps or elsewhere. The sad fact was that many of these children were virtually left to fend for themselves among their relatives who would take them into their homes, as they were able. While the flu epidemic was not the only health problem of that period, it certainly brought to light the need for an organized statewide network that could have been better prepared to care for the sick and dying. Through the efforts of a few people in the state and the assistance of the United States Public Health Services, the governor of New Mexico finally signed the bill that created the state's first Public Health agency in April 1919.

Following the results of the influenza pandemic, a few public and private groups became concerned about the poor health rural people were enduring. This became an issue in which various women's clubs and organizations, mainly in Albuquerque and Santa Fe, played a major role toward improving health services in rural areas. According to Sandra Schackel, these were white, middle-class reformers anxious to impose Progressive Era values on a very diverse, multi-lingual, conservative, rural population. These communities were unaccustomed to strangers asking personal questions about very private matters in their lives. As stated earlier, these well-meaning strangers lacked the trust and the communication skills the local *curanderas* had in their communities.

In Cuba and its surrounding neighboring villages, with few exceptions, our *medicas* and *parteras* continued to deliver most of the babies who were born at home. They also continued to take care of our other ailments using traditional practices well into the late 1940s. We know this is true because there is local folklore involving three families who lived in the same hamlet known then as *Gonzalitos*. Among the different versions of this story, three of the women in this particular neighborhood were in labor, each needing the services of the midwife at the same time. According to the version of this story that I am most familiar with, Doña Gregorita, the midwife who lived closest to this neighborhood, ran from one house to another trying to determine which of the women was furthest along in her labor so she could be present to deliver the baby. Doña Gregorita was probably fully aware of what an old-time obstetrician I once knew used to tell his classes of soon-to-be obstetric nurses and doctors: "with God and women, all things are possible". Given her experiences, this midwife had not ruled out any possibility as it related to her three patients. As it turned out, all three of the women delivered baby boys on the same day. They are two years younger than me and all three are alive and as well as anyone of our age can be.

Keeping in mind that, although the intricacies of germ theory may not have been well understood by the *curanderas* even though it was well known elsewhere and had been studied and practiced since 1870–1875, a traditional folk healer practiced with extreme caution. Their knowledge of medicinal herbs as well as that "extrasensory perception" mentioned earlier allowed them to succeed, barring unforeseen complications.

Curanderia was not limited to traditional folk healers in our remote villages. Every *abuelita* (grandmother) or head of household had their own stock of herbal and other well-known remedies on hand. These people had no other alternatives available to them when someone in the family became sick or injured. If a child woke up with an upset stomach or a light fever, the knowing grandmother would immediately make a batch of *canela* (cinnamon) tea. According to Michael Moore, cinnamon tea is known to "settle and relax the stomach" As well the hot tea will usually help break a fever, especially with a little a*jenjibre* (ginger) added. Neither ginger nor cinnamon is native to our part of the world. Given their effectiveness in folk medicine, however, people here were willing to invest in at least a few of these remedies in an effort to keep their families as healthy as possible. In *A Country Herbal*, Lesley Gordon states that although ginger is a native to Asia it has been one of the most important trade items of the Far East since antiquity. As early as the sixteenth century, Spanish explorers had already brought ginger to America. Our folk healers and people around them knew that having such a valuable product available in their homes was in the interest of their family's health and wellbeing. Similarly, *clavo* (clove) is also not native to the greater southwest but like cinnamon and ginger, its effective uses made it an essential element in folk medicine as well as in our culinary practices.

Even *manzanilla* (chamomile), which was one of the medicinal staples in northern New Mexico, is not native to our area. Given the de-scriptions of how prolific chamomile grew in England, I assume it reached the southwest through trade with the English very early on. Chamomile was also known to grow in immense quantities in places like Italy, Hungry and Poland. My own theory is, given Poland's harsh climate and short growing season, if *manzanilla* could grow in Poland, it could also grow here in Cuba. As a child, I clearly recall *manzanilla* growing in every garden in town. Today, I gather it is grown for commercial purposes here in New Mexico, since one can buy it locally. "*Manzanilla* is a virtual panacea for any disorder accompanied by stomach ache and sleeplessness," says author Michael Moore.

Among our most commonly used native medicinal plants that I would put in the same category as *manzanilla*, are *yerba buena* (mint), *poleo* (downy mint), *oregano* and *osha*. *Cota* (Navajo/Hopi tea), *cañutillo* (Mormon tea) and *chamiso* (saltbush, rabbit brush, or sagebrush) are still used widely for many purposes. Over many years of experience, people have learned the properties and reputations these medicinal plants possess. We also know these plants have been tried, tested and are trusted along with many other native plants that are readily available to us at little or no cost. Different from *Última* and our old *curanderas* and grandmothers, today's generation of local young people is not willing to take the time to learn to recognize, gather and prepare these local treasures. Interestingly, young urban adults who subscribe to natural foods and natural remedies are buying and using these same herbs in shops in nearby cities. In many cases, we would probably be as likely to heal our wounds, our headaches and even our anxieties as successfully with these remedies as we do with all the pills, lineaments and ointments we pay for to make the pharmaceutical companies wealthier than they already are. Furthermore, we want instant results from our medications and as well, we have lost the belief that these herbs and roots can really cure our illnesses.

Like Anaya's *Última*, our folk healers and grandmothers did three things for us in the past that today most of us are not willing to do. They passed down knowledge from people who had practiced before them and added to that store of experiences with what they had learned. They also took the time to locate the places where these valuable plants flourished and they harvested them at the right time and stored them with great care. Most importantly, they respected the natural properties of these plants, using them with extreme caution and skill at appropriate times with a select clientele, knowing that these remedies were not for everyone. Today, there is still much we could learn, given the information available from our folk healers. This is especially the case given how uncertain the wellbeing of our planet and its resources appear to be, which could well determine our future health care. Under no circumstances must the knowledge base of our former *curanderas, medicas* and *sobadores* be underestimated or referred to as "quackery". As advanced as modern medicine may appear to be to us now, and as dependent as so many of us are on our medical practitioners, there is still time for us to learn from our incredibly rich past. Let us not forget our nearest hospital is still eighty miles away. Our roads may be better than in the past but inclement weather can still determine whether even Medivac can serve us, due to our isolated location. Perhaps *Última's* and grandma's old *remedios* are still worth learning about, even in the high-tech world of the twenty-first century.

Una Plática en Memoria de Juan Rafael
(A Conversation about a Special Person)

This *Plática* is about a special person who once lived in our little village of Cuba. There is an adage commonly attributed to the ancient Chinese that says, "It takes a whole village to raise a child." Many years ago, the village of Cuba raised a child who grew up to be the man called Juan Rafael. He was not homeless or without a family. His family lived and worked in our community just like all the rest of us did. However, they could not always take care of Juan Rafael in the traditional way because he was mentally disabled and would not stay at home. He preferred to be outdoors more than anywhere else and spent virtually all his time wandering around Cuba and nearby areas.

The people of the village were aware that Juan Rafael's family simply could not keep up with him. Try as they might, they were simply unable to provide the constant care that he needed. By the time I became aware of Juan Rafael, his widowed mother was elderly and lived alone, a place where Juan Rafael was rarely seen. His siblings also lived in town and tried to help their mother care for Juan Rafael but they had families of their own with the usual obligations related to jobs and earning a living.

The people of Cuba, especially the women and children, took care of Juan Rafael when his family could not. He roamed aimlessly through the pastures and vacant fields and might stand idle for hours or otherwise move along in some undeterminable direction at his own pace. He roamed freely in a territory that extended from *Las Lagunitas* (now the area south of town between Highway 197 and Highway 550) north beyond the schools and almost up to Los Pinos. Amazingly, the local dogs did not bother him, children did not taunt, jeer or mock him in any way nor did anyone interfere with his migration from one end of his territory to the other.

If a family got up in the morning and Juan Rafael was already standing out in the middle of their pasture that would have been noted.

If he were still there when they were ready to sit down and eat, one of the children would be sent out either to bring Juan Rafael in to eat or to take him something to eat and drink in the field.

In the extreme dry heat of summer, if Juan Rafael were standing out in the open without a hat, a mother would send one of her children out to take him into a shaded area or at least to take him a hat and give him some water.

In winter, whenever Juan Rafael might be standing outside seemingly unaware of the cold, wind or snow, someone in a family would go get him and bring him into their house, feed him, dry him and in some cases, bathe him and dress him in warm, dry clothes. This was done because everyone knew that he was oblivious to the most essential requirements for human survival in our generally cold and unpredictable winter weather.

On some occasions, especially in winter, Juan Rafael stayed with a family for several days at a time. Then he would be asked to help with the chores. Even given his short attention span, he was capable of chopping wood and bringing in kindling. He could haul water under supervision and even help with the feeding of animals for a brief time. People generally treated him with kindness and he must have known in some way where the sanctuaries for survival were located. Like migratory birds, he would return to these safe havens during his wanderings. The best anyone could do was to reassure his mother that someone between Las Lagunitas, Cubita and the northernmost end of Cuba had taken him in and that he was safe.

It is true that Juan Rafael lived in our community a long time ago and since then Cuba has evolved into a more modern community. Yet, as the parent of a mentally disabled son, I can attest that during the twenty years that my son Vincent lived here with my mother he also was treated kindly. Some of the same people who had cared for Juan Rafael a generation earlier raised the quality of Vincent's life well above what it had been in the urban environment where he spent his early childhood. That urban experience was a source of tremendous stress and dislocation for him and his immediate family. When Vincent came here to live with my mother in 1980, he did not stand out in the middle of a field for hours at a time but there were occasions when he would wander short distances. His behavior was abnormal enough that people in this community intervened on his behalf with kindness, generosity and humanity.

Most importantly, like Juan Rafael's family, we who are Vincent's family had the assurance from friends and neighbors that he would always be safe. As well, there were our long-term law officers such as Joseph Gurulé, Gabe Romero and Johnny Wiese who knew Vincent and assured us that, if necessary, they would act in his behalf. This sort of support came from people in all walks of life, including some of the so-called "street people." Some of these people who roam our streets observe every move and hear every plan and probably have a greater understanding of what is going on than many of the rest of us. I was personally told by one such person that he would not let anything bad ever happen to Vincent.

Although there were no members of Juan Rafael's family in Cuba in 2014 when I first wrote this piece as an article for the Cuba News, I felt I should at least make the family aware that this story was going to be told. I was able to contact a nephew of Juan Rafael and got consent before submitting the story to the newspaper.

I also learned from the family that Juan Rafael had died some time in the early 1950s at the State Mental Hospital in Las Vegas. By that time, his elderly mother had died. The one older brother that had been living here was moving to Albuquerque. In the absence of family in the area, Juan Rafael's days of roaming freely in and around Cuba came to an end.

By that time, Cuba had become part of twentieth-century America and not much notice would have been paid to the death of a man who evoked kindness and generosity in the village that helped raise him and look after him through his entire life. As for Vincent, he has been in a facility in Santa Fé since 2001. He participates in a program that is dedicated to providing services and activities for adults such as himself and people like Juan Rafael.

Today there are few of us alive who still remember Juan Rafael or the fact that in his time there were few if any health services for those of us who were relatively healthy, much less for people with special needs. Juan Rafael might very well have benefitted from such services, had they existed. But the people of Cuba, with its meager resources made sure that

Juan Rafael was always safe, adequately fed and properly clothed.

Caring for each other is not "Rocket Science." However, it is a way for communities such as ours to survive in good times as well as the lean and difficult times. Back in the days when Juan Rafael's elderly mother was unable to care for her special man-child, this community proved that it took a whole village to make his life secure and showed that we were capable of caring for this person with such special needs. The result was that we were a better village for having done so.

Perhaps our "street people" should also be looked upon more kindly and treated with more respect. Instead, people fear that they will steal everything out of their cars while they are shopping if they do not lock their cars. They walk by without speaking as if these "street people" did not even exist. Like my Vincent and Juan Rafael a generation earlier, there are many people in our community that we see as being different from ourselves. How we treat all of these people determines what kind of a community we are.

Cuba and other small towns like it are places where people have known their neighbors and their cousins for generations. We generally know who people are, how they are related to each other and at least some details of their lives. We know that we are connected and that we are cared about.

The generous way our forebears interacted with Juan Rafael and the kindness and tolerance that people more recently demonstrated towards Vincent and other disabled people in our community illustrate "the rules which the community has evolved for its own protection." These rules bond us as a community in ways that are different from people living in urban areas. There are places we may know of personally and certainly hear about where even normal children cannot play outdoors without adult supervision for fear that something tragic will happen to them. Those places are not safe because their citizens are not well connected to each other. They are often not aware of other people's disabilities or misfortunes or even the ordinary events of their neighbors' lives.

There is no doubt that even for a village such as Cuba, Juan Rafael was an oddity and by now some readers may be wondering why people took care of him. I believe the answer lies in a quote ascribed to the author W. Somerset Maugham. In one of his stories he says, "Conscience is the guardian in the individual of the rules which the community has evolved for its own protection." In other words, there is a conscious awareness, perhaps even a fear that if one of us or a member of our family were to be found in a situation similar to that of Juan Rafael, we would want that person treated humanely, kindly and with dignity. Such awareness bonds people together to care for each other and thereby determines what kind of community we become.

Los Genízaros de la Frontera
(The Peoples of New Spain's Frontier)

Today the term Genízaro(a) is a nearly forgotten word among the Spanish speaking population of northern New Mexico and southern Colorado. Yet the word itself has had an improbable history and an evolution that began in the fourteenth century. The term Genízaro is derived from the Turkish language as "Yaniceri" or "Janissary" meaning "new troops." Following the reconquest of New Mexico in 1693, it was used to designate a group of Native American people living during New Mexico's colonial period and beyond. The designation of this class of people known as Genízaros is one of the historical events that distinguish northern New Mexicans from many other Hispanics in the southwestern United States.

It is my perception that historically the people who were defined as Genízaros have had the greatest social and genealogical impact on who we, the *Norteños* (northern New Mexicans) are as a people today. We are the descendants of Genízaros as well as of our Spanish ancestors. Even though on occasion one may hear someone claim that he or she is of pure Spanish heritage, history proves otherwise. The Celts, Arabs, Basques and Jews among others were all a part of our heritage even before our "pure Spanish" ancestors left Europe to colonize the western hemisphere. Yet, for some people throughout northern New Mexico and southern Colorado there seems to be the implication that being of pure Spanish heritage is somehow better than having Genízaros as ancestors as well. It is this difference in attitude that is among the *pláticas* (conversations) whose time has come to be understood.

At a personal level, I have had a long association with the term Genízara and over the years developed a great interest in its meaning and implications. As a small child growing up in Cuba, my paternal grandfather, Don Francisco Cordova, always referred to me as "la Genízara." I do not recall that he ever called me anything else. Since I had no idea what the term meant, I simply grew up assuming it was an unusual term of endearment that was applied only to me by my grandfather.

It was not until I started studying New Mexico history that I realized what grandpa was calling me or the implications of the term. According to Rubén Cobos' *Dictionary of New Mexico and Southern Colorado Spanish,* a Genízaro is the "offspring of non-European parents of mixed blood. A non-Pueblo Indian captive rescued by the Spanish settlers from various nomadic tribes." As an adjective, it also meant "dark skinned." What was astounding to me later in life was that my grandfather called me Genízara in front of my parents and, as far as I can recall, neither of my parents ever objected. Perhaps they also thought it was an unusual term of endearment and we can now give them both the benefit of the doubt.

The early Spaniards who migrated into the northern-most reaches of the Spanish Empire in the dawn of New Mexico's colonial period obviously brought this term with them from Spain. As situations arose in their new environment similar to their previous experiences, they must have simply found the term useful and applied it accordingly.

According to some New Mexican authors, the term Genízaro was applied originally to disenfranchised Pueblo people who had become Christianized and assimilated into Spanish communities. These Pueblo people were often expelled from their homes and banished from their tribes because of the association with the Spanish settlers.

As colonization continued and expanded, especially through the eighteenth century, the number of Plains people captured, kidnapped or sold increased tremendously. These Plains people were traded primarily by the Comanches and the Utes to the Spanish for horses, sheep, wool blankets, corn and corn meal. The captive people were put to work in the homes of the Spanish settlers and in the missions as maids, sheepherders and farm hands. They would immediately be baptized in the Catholic Church, given Spanish names and usually the surnames of the families that took them in. The church records would list them as Christians and thereby members of a household to be raised in the Spanish fashion. In Spanish, they were known as *criados,* meaning they had been brought up in the household to be servants. The verb *criar* means to rear, to bring up or raise which is what families did when they bought a *criado*.

The military used some captives as scouts, interpreters and as soldiers. In the military context, the term Genízaro is roughly consistent with the original Turkish term, "Janissary." During the expansion of the Turkish Empire, the Sultan needed more troops. Many of these additional troops were conscripted from Christian families in the Balkans, required to adopt the Muslim faith and were soldiers for the rest of their lives. They were considered the property of the Sultan and even served as his bodyguards. Even though this happened a hundred years before the Spanish began to come to the New World, the term remained in the Spanish vocabulary. It was used first by Spanish soldiers and later by settlers as they spread out over the frontier.

In New Mexico, the Genízaros were not forced to be in the military for life but they did become the new troops the settlers needed to ward off the constant threat of attack from neighboring nomadic tribes.

By 1754, there were so many Genízaros in northern New Mexico that Governor Vélez Cachupin established the first Genízaro land grant at Abiquiu. The grantees were a group of Plains Natives from various tribes along with some Hopis and Tewas. Many of the grantees had formerly been servants of the Spanish and would have been Christianized. These Genízaros of various tribes and backgrounds were now officially recognized as the owners of the Pueblo of Abiquiu land grant. Under Spanish law, the people were provided with an ample water supply, sufficient land for agriculture and an *ejido*, or common land for grazing as well as woodlands for gathering fuel.

Between 1754 and the early 1800s, Abiquiu became one of northern New Mexico's most successful illegal trade centers. Under Spanish law it was forbidden to trade with anyone from outside the Empire, including the Plains tribe, French trappers and Americans. All trade was to go through Santa Fé southward into Chihuahua, Zacatecas and Mexico City. Abiquiu, being so far north and such a long way from the enforcement of law, flourished as a center of unregulated and often illegal trade. Abiquiu was officially occupied by people of different tribes who spoke different native languages as well as Spanish, which made commerce less complicated and very profitable for all parties concerned.

Following 1821, when Mexico won its independence from Spain, the new government opened its borders to all kinds of trade. The famous Santa Fé trail between St. Louis, Missouri and Santa Fé was an outgrowth of this new trade policy. The Mexican government also relaxed the laws that related to where people could settle, travel and trade.

New Mexico settlers immediately pushed northward toward the San Luis Valley, now in southern Colorado because of its prime agricultural land. Efforts to settle by these people were repeatedly repelled by fierce attacks by Comanche and Ute warriors. The San Luis Valley was the home of a band of Utes and surrounding areas were considered sacred lands. They fought mightily to defend their lands against the would-be Spanish settlers. Abiquiu became the safe hub for the various waves of settlers whose attempts to settle in the San Luis Valley failed.

Abiquiu was well fortified and located on a defensible mesa with its own garrison of soldiers. Some of the survivors of the San Luis Valley adventures stayed around Abiquiu only temporarily. Others remained in or around Abiquiu and never left their Genízaro neighbors, friends and cousins. Some of these people migrated westward to form the communities of Coyote, Gallina and Capulín and some even crossed over into the upper Rio Puerco valley to join the already developing communities of San José (now Regina), La Jara and Nacimiento (now Cuba).

Historically, as Genízaros gained resources of their own, they were allowed to become landowners. They remained in the Catholic church. Having met these criteria, they were allowed to marry into Spanish families and were then referred to as *vecinos*. In Spanish, a *vecino* is a neighbor. *Vecinos* had higher social status then *Genízaros*. However, on many church records, the priests continued to describe a marriage as being that of a *vecino* and a Spanish mate. The truth was that these former Genízaros became completely assimilated into mainstream society. Having been given Spanish baptismal names as well as Spanish surnames from families they originally served, eventually there was no way to distinguish between Genízaros, Vecinos or pure Spaniards. It is probably for this reason that the term Genízaro has disappeared from our vocabulary and vecino has reverted to its original meaning.

The irony in this story of my grandfather calling me Genízara, I later discovered, is that he was right. I do have Genízara ancestry and no one knew about this particular part of my ancestry better than he. The story began back in the mid-nineteenth century, following Mexican independence from Spain in 1821. This is when Spanish restrictions on trade and where people could reside were done away with. Under the more liberal Mexican laws, people could move and live wherever they wanted without official permission.

Among the people trying to relocate and hopefully prosper in the far reaches of the province were two brothers, Antonio and Pascual Cordova. Early on, they were believed to be living in Taos. They were among the many settlers who had migrated north from the middle Rio Grande Valley waiting for an eventual opportunity to move into the San Luis Valley, now in southern Colorado.

While living in Taos, the two Cordova brothers married descendants of an old French family known as Jáquez. Pascual married Maria Dolores Jáquez and Antonio married her sister, Maria Ignacita Jáquez. Together these brothers and their wives joined one of several large groups of prospective settlers determined to lay claim to a part of the lush, fertile San Luis Valley.

The particular group of ambitious New Mexicans the Cordova brothers had joined actually succeeded. Some among them, including the Cordovas, got a foothold on land along Culebra Creek, west of the present-day town of San Luis in Costilla County. They were able to maintain a presence there at least until the mid-1870s before the Utes, with some help from their neighbors, drove the New Mexicans back down to Abiquiu again.

The 1880 census taken in the communities of Gallina and Capulín, shows that many of the families the Cordova brothers had accompanied to the Culebra Creek area were now back in these New Mexico communities. Antonio and Pascual had probably gone to the Culebra Creek area as early as the 1860s, since the census records show that Pascual's three oldest children were born there between 1866 and 1873. The fourth child, Julian, was born in 1875 and is listed as having been born in Coyote, as were two younger brothers, Juan Francisco (my grandfather) and Marino. Coyote is only "a stone's throw" away from Capulín and Gallina and a few miles upstream from Abiquiu.

Among the Spanish settlers who also ventured into the San Luis Valley were the family of Rafael Lucero and his wife, Josefita. Interestingly, no last name is recorded for her. They had a son named José Nacario who was married to Avelina Aragon. While attempting to establish themselves in the San Luis Valley, they had a son named Manuel Reyes Lucero who was born in Conejos. Conejos is a settlement located on the Conejos River just north of the present-day community of Antonito, Colorado. According to his diary, Manuel Reyes had lived with his grandparents, Rafael and Josefita in Conejos since he was a very young child.

Manuel Reyes wrote that when he was thirteen years old, his grand-father Rafael died. Following this death, his father, José Nacario, brought Manuel Reyes to Cuba and took grandmother Josefita, at her request, to Cochiti Pueblo. BINGO! Why would Nacario take his mother to Cochiti if she were not a member of that Pueblo community?

In his diary, Manuel Reyes Lucero continues to describe the steps he took in caring for his grandmother Josefita. He reports that after spending some time in Cochiti, Josefita asked Manuel Reyes to bring her to Cuba. Manuel Reyes does not specify how long Josefita was in Cochiti before she asked him to bring her to Cuba. It is possible that she was no longer welcome among her own people, having been married to a Hispanic. Given that she died only six years after her husband, she could not have stayed at Cochiti very long. He brought her to Cuba and cared for her until she "passed to a better life" in 1881. At that time, Manuel Reyes was nineteen years old. In October of 1884, Manuel Reyes Lucero married Teresita Montoya. They were one of the families I wrote about earlier who had six female children and no male heirs. The oldest of these daughters, Leonor, married "none other than" Juan Francisco Cordova, my grandfather.

Having married Leonor, Francisco would have known that his father-in-law, Manuel Reyes, had Pueblo ancestors, as would his wife and others in the family. However, I do not recall that he called any of my cousins Genízaros, even though we had the same grandmother and her lineage. Recall that among the definitions Ruben Cobos provides for Genízara is "dark skinned." Perhaps I was the darkest of his grandchildren and that was the reason for the name.

I have not had my DNA analyzed. I keep thinking about it but haven't and may not need to. Recently, my son, Aaron May, had his DNA analyzed and was told that fourteen percent of his heritage was Native American. Since his father likely had no Native American heritage, I should be about twenty-eight percent Native American. Other sources suggest that the average Native American heritage of northern New Mexico Hispanics is actually slightly higher than that. Given the high degree of intermarriage within a community that stretches from southern Colorado to central New Mexico, it would probably be difficult to find any Hispanic who has no Native American heritage.

I believe that the Genízaros in our past have had a very positive impact on who we are as a people. They have helped to determine the foods we eat, the traditional medicinal herbs we still use and, perhaps, a part of the way we look at life.

The fact is that we have a wonderful mix of numerous European, Middle Eastern and Native American bloodlines, all of which make us unique but also bonded to a very large part of the human population. I am happy as well as proud to have such a diverse and generally healthy genealogy.

Don Francisco Cordova con la Genízara del Norte (author), 1937.

El Idioma de la Plática Local
(The Language of Local Conversation)

Traditional northern New Mexico and southern Colorado Spanish as I have written about before is neither standard nor academically "proper" Spanish. Our long history of isolation from The Mother Tongue has left us a lot of opportunity to adjust the language to our own needs and to fit it to our own environment. Some would say we have debased and degraded the language. Personally, I think we have been rather creative in the use of the language we inherited from common soldiers, farmers, herdsmen and our Native neighbors. The few educated priests that came here would have had less influence than the *comadre* (respected neighbor, God-mother) next door on how we should pronounce the archaic words left behind by our colonial ancestors. Today you do not have to be a linguist to understand why speakers of modern standard Spanish frequently have difficulty understanding Spanish speakers from this area. The situation is not much different from those who still speak something more like the language of Shakespeare's time in the hill country of the eastern United States or the Cajun speakers of Louisiana or eastern Canada. In each case, isolation has led to holding on to old expressions and making up new ones that suited our needs. It is simply part of our history and inheritance.

The terms and phrases selected for this chapter are but few from the vast number of non-standard Spanish terms used locally in casual conversation. These will include archaic words, and some rather confusing words. I will include some words in which letters were interchanged as well as made up words and phrases and a few anglicized words. I am not including any *pachuquismos,* the language originally used by the "zoot-suiters" in the urban areas of the southwest. There are now highly scholarly works available in this field of linguistics that have done a better job than I could ever hope to do. Besides, *pachuquismos* were not widely used among the people of this rural area.

For years, I have been collecting words and phrases that were in common use here in Cuba and our neighboring communities that I never heard in other Spanish-speaking environments. Furthermore, when I used some of these words in my travels among standard Spanish speakers, I would get a reaction that was either one of surprise, disbelief or simply a failure to understand what I was trying to say. For example, I used an archaic word, *atrancar*. Here the word means to lock a door, window or gate. We still use this word in rural New Mexico. In earlier times, this term meant to secure an opening with a cross bar. While I was in Spain some years ago, I once asked a porter, *"¿Atranco la puerta, señor?"* I only meant to ask if he had locked the door to my hotel room. The porter stopped dead in his tracks and turned to me to ask where I had learned that word. He told me he had not heard that word used since before his great-grandmother died! For speakers of standard Spanish, you would now say *cerrar con llave* (to close with a key).

When you consider our history and the fact that our early settlements were under assault well into the nineteenth century, we literally had to bar the doors, windows and gates and hope that they were secure enough to discourage any potential invader. *Cerrar con llave* (close with a key) would not have done us much good in those times when we were under attack!

Among the most common archaic words used locally are words which were modernized for most of the Spanish-speaking world by the *Real Academia Española* (The Royal Academy of the Spanish Language.) long after our ancestors left Spain. The *Academia* is made up of language scholars from all over the Spanish-speaking world who meet periodically to update the Spanish language. They decide whether a word meets all the rules to be a "Spanish" word and if so, it is included in the next edition of the Royal Academy's Dictionary. These dictionaries are massive and were published every ten years following endless meetings and debates in the Academy. Most of this standardization occurred after the early settlers of the New World left Spain. It is obvious that New Mexico Spanish was left behind and that New Mexico Spanish-speakers were not represented in the *Real Academia Española*.

Because of our isolation, we have come to use words differently from standard Spanish speakers. For example, *Túnico* is derived from the Spanish word *túnica,* which describes a sleeveless garment more like an ancient tunic or toga. In standard Spanish, the modern word for such a garment is *vestido.* Locally we regard a *vestido* as a suit, especially a two- or three-piece suit worn by either a man or a woman. Here, *túnico* means a woman's dress.

Another archaic word we still use commonly is *fierro,* which in standard Spanish becomes *hierro* (with a silent "h") and is translated as iron. What is interesting about this word is that in Portuguese, a language that evolved from Spanish, they use the word *ferro* for iron. I suspect that originally the Spanish word was the same as the Portuguese and somewhere along the way it was changed to its modern spelling. Nobody told us about that in New Mexico!

As recently as 2015, I came to realize how well we have retained some of our ancient vocabulary. A visiting rancher from a nearby town was relating a story about having sold a bull to a friend but the friend did not pay for the bull right away. Our friend later asked him if he was going to keep the bull and the other rancher said he wanted the bull. At this time, our friend responded by saying, "¡*Pues Shekalella!*" (well, pay up!). Our friend was using a version of the term *shekel,* which was the standard silver coin of the ancient Hebrews and Babylonians and came to mean "money" in medieval Spain.

I believe that, given the centuries-old relationship between Jews, Arabs and Spaniards in Spain (before 1492), the word *shekel* was brought to Mexico by our earliest colonial ancestors and there are those among us who still use such terms today. (Our earliest ancestors came to the New World within a hundred years after both Jews and Moors were expelled from Spain.)

A different kind of problem is illustrated by the word *nutria.* If you look at a map of northern New Mexico, there are many creeks, streams and lakes named *Nutria.* As well, there are five places called *Nutrina.* According to Robert Julyan, author of *The Place Names of New Mexico, nutria* means otter in standard Spanish When the Spanish colonists first saw the

North American beaver, an otter-like animal, they gave it the same name. In northern New Mexico, *nutria* generally mean beaver rather than otter and that is what it means in our place names. This is an example of the "confused words" that we use. The diagram below illustrates some of these words.

local word	true meaning	local meaning	standard Spanish
nutria	otter	beaver	*castor*
nodriza	child's nurse	hospital nurse	*enfermera*
chino	Chinese	curl	*rizo*
tiro	team of horses	team of players	*equipo*
avispa	wasp	bee	*abeja*

Locally, when we are speaking about a nurse in a hospital, we should say *enfermera,* a word that has never found its way into our vocabulary. We still refer to someone with curly hair as being *chino.* The word *rizo* again is never used here in that context. Long ago, when people had teams of horses, I recall that we referred to such a team as *un tiro de caballos,* which is the correct use of the term. When or why we started using the word to refer to a sports team I do not know. What I am sure of is that the term *equipo* as a sport team I learned as an adult. I had never used the word nor do I believe I ever heard that word used around here.

When I was in kindergarten, I was stung on the thumb by a wasp. Being highly allergic to wasps, my thumb swelled up horribly. The very concerned kindergarten Sister asked me what had happened and my reply was that I had been "bitten by a bus." The sympathetic Sister (who spoke no Spanish) could not figure out what kind of a "bus" could have bitten me so she called for one of my aunts who was a few grades ahead of me. I explained to my aunt what had happened and she told the Sister that I had been stung by a wasp. The Sister asked where the "bus" came into the story and I said, "buzz, buzz: what bit me was going buzz-buzz." Obviously, I did not yet know the English word for *avispa.*

As for the difference between a wasp and a bee, normally we do call wasps, or yellow jackets, *avispas*. Bees, on the other hand, we call *cormenas*, which we also use to refer to bumblebees. We rarely use the word *abeja* to refer to bees. What is interesting about the word *cormena* is that I have not found a single reference to such a word, especially related to bees or bumblebees. Bumblebee is translated as *abejorro* or *abejón*. Apparently, we made up the word *cormena* or possibly borrowed it from a language other than Spanish.

In regard to the following category of words, standard Spanish-speakers cringe when they hear how we have interchanged letters to give these words a completely different sound which they cannot understand. Others of these they simple refer to as *barbarismos*, barbaric assaults on the sacredness of the Spanish language of the *Academia*. Again, this list is long and one I find especially interesting.

The first of these words I will describe are two names. For reasons long lost in our isolation, we have changed Gabriel into *Grabiel*. Women have not been spared, for the female version of this name is *Grabielita*. Interestingly, if we speak of a man in Spanish, he is referred to as *Grabiel* but if the conversation is in English, he is usually Gabriel or just Gabe. The same is true for women. The other name used here was *Pelegrino* which probably ought to be *Peregrino*. The latter means pilgrim or traveler. How the spelling and pronunciation of this name changed I have no idea.

We call a wall a *pader*, while the correct form is *pared*. To this day I still find it difficult to say *pared* instead of *pader*. The next two words I believe we simply rewrote to our own liking. The word *redepente*, which means suddenly and is used often is supposed to be *de repente*. The next one I can understand how we would abuse. Not having much access to theatres, what difference would it have made to us, in olden times, how it was properly pronounced. Now we really have to learn to say *teatro* (theatre) instead of *treato*. Then also, there is the word *abuja* (needle), which should be *aguja*. Try convincing grandma that *aguja* is really the correct word. Good luck! Furthermore, dear readers, can you understand why standard Spanish-speakers and well-meaning Spanish teachers are puzzled when they hear us say *chiquete* (gum) instead of *chicle?*

Among some of my favorite names and phrases used locally to describe people are words like *desclavada*. Colloquially speaking a female that was called this was being told she was offset, off-center or simply off her rocker or being extremely silly. In literal translation, this means the nails have been removed or are missing. Sort of related to *desclavada* is the term *escariota*. This is a show-off but loud and silly. While if someone was called *faceta*, they would be described as a conceited, vain and uppity snob. Now a *safao* should be a slipshod, negligent person but again, colloquially, it was someone who had "slipped their chain," someone with no sense at all.

Peseta, according to Ruben Cobos, is a euphemism for *pesado*, someone who is dull, boring and disagreeable. We would say of such a person *me cae pesado* (I find him boring, dull. etc.). This use of the word is interesting because the *peseta* was Spain's monetary unit until it joined the European Union. In the Colonial and Territorial periods, a peseta was a silver coin worth two *reales*, or twenty-five cents. Up until the mid-twentieth century, people here still counted their money in *reales*. *Dos reales* was equal to twenty-five cents; *cuatro reales* was equal to fifty cents, *seis reales* was equal to seventy-five cents and finally a *peso* was equal to a dollar.

This leads me to one of my favorite phrases, *Ha Fulano le falta un real para el peso*. Literally this means that a person (*Fulano*) doesn't know the difference between a *real* (twelve and a half cents) and a *peso* (dollar). Locally it meant that the person was "slow on the draw," or not all there.

A category of words that are commonly used locally in conversations we borrowed so early in our colonial history we simply assume they are Spanish. In truth, we have perpetuated a long list of our vocabulary borrowed from the *Náhuatl* language, the language of the Aztec people and other people in central Mexico into our everyday language because we had no other appropriate words. A *metate* was a stone used for grinding corn. Neither corn nor *metates* were known is Spain. A *comal* was the flat stone on which tortillas were cooked. When metal became available, we replaced the stone with a flat metal sheet. *Ocote*, is a type of pine tree we know as pitch pine. In *Náhuatl*, it would be *ocotl*. We all know that *ocote* was the desired wood for heating our homes in winter. In early spring, everyone's favorite complaint is mud. The word we use to describe this nuisance is *zoquete*." Certainly, our early ancestors knew about mud from Spain but dropped the term *barro* in favor of the *Náhuatl* term, *zoquete*.

From *Náhuatl*, we also borrowed the word *zacate*, which means grass. Local ranchers describe alfalfa hay, used for feeding cows, horses and sheep as containing either a little or a lot of *zacate*. No word of Spanish origin is used here for grass. A particular species of grass is called *popotón*. This utilitarian staple was very relevant to local populations. When cut and dried, *popotón* was used to make brooms. Locally, we referred to the brooms as *escobas de popóte*.

From *Náhuatl*, we also inherited the word *mecate*, which means fiber rope. Locally, however, we use this word in our local vernacular to mean everything from a shoestring to a rope. We made this word fit every variety of Spanish word from *cordón* (cord), to *cuerda* (a small whip), *cuenda* (the end of a skein of silk or yarn) and *cabresto*, which is also a native borrowed word meaning a heavy rope.

Early Spanish immigrants adopted many *Náhuatl* words to describe plants and animals they had not encountered before. For example, while there are dogs and wolves both in Europe and the Americas, we have something else here. It is generally larger than a dog and smaller than a wolf. The *Náhuatl* word for this animal is *coyotl* and we call them coyotes. There are owls in Spain but they are different from most owls here. Thus, owls are called *tecolotes* instead of *lechuza*. There are no turkeys in Europe so they took on the *Náhuatl* name of *guajolotl*, or *guajolote* in New Mexico Spanish. The list of *Náhuatl* words in our vocabulary is long and springs from a close relationship with Native people in Mexico over a long time before coming north. Among the many other words, we use are ajalote (water dog), *tapushque (loft)*, *tapanco* (mound or heap) and *guaje* (baby's rattle). It is important to note that other Spanish speakers have had much more contact with people from other areas and have ceased to use some of these terms. Because of our isolation, we still use them.

From our local Native neighbors, the Tewa people, we borrowed the place name *Chimayó*, originally *Tsimajo*, which has several interesting meanings. Primarily, it means obsidian flake. It also became the name for a type of blanket. These blankets are differentiated from a Navajo woven blanket by the type of loom that they were woven on and by the designs. Among the Tewa people, *Chimayó* also meant a detribalized Indian or a *Genízaro*. These people also gave us the word *tegua* (pronounced like Tewa), which translates to moccasins for Spanish speakers in New Mexico. In this case we probably took the name of the Tewa people from whom we learned to make *teguas*. *Teguas* would have been far more practical than *abarcas*, which the Spanish would have been familiar with. These were basically a leather sole with thongs and loops that would wrap around the foot. After all, those boots made of beautiful Spanish leather would not have lasted very long. Winters were longer and colder in the northern frontier and *teguas* must have seemed like a great way to solve an ongoing need.

Without some intervention, however, this rich linguistic heritage may soon be lost. All our children and grandchildren may become mono-lingual English speakers and they will not even say, *voy a baquiar mi troca*, when they are telling you they are backing up their truck. It is possible that they will still ask you if you could *sainear un cheque* (sign a check) to hold them over until payday. For those who want to prevent this and preserve our unique dialect, there are resources available.

As early as 1966 a teacher in the Deming, New Mexico Public Schools by the name of Pauline Baker recognized that teaching modern standard Spanish to Hispanics who already spoke the language was different from teaching Spanish as a second language. Ms. Baker wrote and published a little book titled *Español Para Los Hispanos* which is an excellent resource for anyone who accepts the reality that we have our own version of the language and we can still improve on how we use it. I recommend Ms. Baker's book if you can find it. Starting as far back as the 1940s, Professor Ruben Cobos began compiling materials for what became *A Dictionary of New Mexico and Southern Colorado Spanish*. This work was first published by the Museum of New Mexico Press in 1983. The revised and expanded revision of 2003 is by far the most authoritative source of our regional dialect to date and is readily available. The dictionary includes origins and usage of every entry. For anyone wishing to learn more about this unique language of ours, I recommend Cobos' work wholeheartedly. Cobos' dictionary gives those of us who have been reprimanded for using Spanish incorrectly confidence and pride in knowing how rich our dialect really is.

Although we call our language Spanish, it is neither modern nor standard. It is colorfully archaic, altered and adapted to our needs and our environment. It has served us well for several centuries and hopefully will serve us for a long time to come. Preserving this part of our heritage is very important to those of us who still enjoy the sounds and phrases we use in our conversations, our *pláticas.*

Escobitas de popote (grass brooms).

Una Plática Sobre los Cambios en Nuestros Modos de Vivir
(A Conversation About Our Community's Life Style Changes)

Following World War II (1941–1945), how did it happen that we as a community gave up our way of life so readily? Was it because we were tired of being "poor?" Was it because we simply did not want to work as hard as our ancestors had done before us? Or was it because so many members of our humble village had been away during the war and discovered how easy it had become to quietly move away from our sacred mountains? They now knew they could go back to California or to Utah where they were aware that there were good-paying jobs. With money they earned, they could buy a car. They might even buy a house with running water, electricity and a bathroom. The truth is that, like so many other people all over the country, we wanted to become part of the new "modern" society.

However, in the process of becoming modern, we lost our language. We forgot how to grow our healthful foods. Our livestock became a burden and eventually many of us even lost our property. Among the most dramatic changes that occurred during this time was the loss of the intimate connection we had with our extended families. Today our "extended" families truly extend throughout the eleven western states, Alaska and even beyond.

Until World War II, that critical point in our history, Cuba and so many other northern New Mexico villages had survived in spite of adverse conditions primarily because of our strong family connections and sound family values. These values were based on the bedrock of what we now call common courtesies. These were a system of polite, considerate acts and respect for all life, for each other and for our common wellbeing. Deviate too far from these values and you would not survive as an individual, a family or a community. We were bonded by our mutual needs and thereby committed to these values.

Although Cuba and many of our surrounding communities were

predominantly Catholic, readers might simply regard these practices as Catholic Church values. Keep in mind, however, that in 2014, the Cuba Presbyterian Church celebrated its 125th. anniversary in this community and there were other religious influences on the community as well. What seems important as it relates to our values is that regardless of religious denomination or church affiliation, these family values were being reinforced in the institutions that mattered most to all local families. The churches and the schools helped promote these values, along with our families.

Among the practices observed by all families in our community was gathering to share meals as often as possible. There were valid reasons why families used to sit together at mealtime. In spite of their meager resources, these people firmly believed they could give thanks and they would say grace when everyone was in place and ready to eat. This seemingly minor practice was not only an act of civility; it assured that every member of the family was being fed and participating in the ritual together. Sharing meals also allowed time to participate in conversations related to the events of the day and address personal as well as family problems that might be important for one or several members of the family. In addition, this time might provide the opportunity to plan and prepare for the next day's work and who would be responsible for each task.

This gathering at table was no less important than the teaching of prayers or going to church. A twentieth-century philosopher named Martin Buber is quoted as saying, "One eats in holiness and the table becomes an altar." Outside of our churches, the family gathering at table was where family values were instilled and reinforced. Buber's statement seems to have been very appropriate to our homes. There is a rhyme in Spanish that discouraged children from being silly at the table that says, *"el que come y canta, loco se levanta."* (He who sits at the table and sings and eats will leave the table weird.) Obviously, none of us wanted to be looked upon as a foolish or crazy person so we behaved at the table.

Other than the meager nourishment we each received, this mealtime was an opportunity for young people to be reminded of who were there *tíos* and *tías*, (uncles and aunts) and who were their *"primos"* (cousins). Getting these relationships right was very important. It was also a time for young people to observe the values of the older members of the family and how their own family went about solving problems and resolving disputes.

Today, I look around restaurants and see two adults talking on their cell phones and children with their heads buried in their favorite electronic gadgets. No one is speaking to any other person around the table. They barely take time to pick up another piece of pizza with one hand while manipulating the phone or toy with the other. I ponder what our kindly, courteous grandparents would think of such disconnection and lack of conversation or courtesy.

Prior to the 1950s, the language spoken at home across generations in Hispanic homes was Spanish. In the 1920s, when the Convent School opened, Spanish was forbidden at school. The non-Spanish-speaking sisters put tremendous pressure on their students to learn English while frequently punishing them for speaking Spanish. This had a huge impact on our attitudes about our native language. By 1936, when the Convent School celebrated its first high school graduation, we had a large group of bilingual Spanish/English speakers. Yet, the language at home was still predominantly Spanish.

Between World War II and 1950 (only about five years), we began to see a real change in the dominance of English over Spanish both at home as well as out in the community. The number of English speaking young people began to create a significant breach between the older Spanish-speaking members of the family and the younger members. The younger people seemed not to want to be associated with the older people or the old ways. Speaking Spanish was thought of as being obsolete, not "cool." Furthermore, many of the parents of this generation did not want their children to go through the humiliation of speaking Spanish in school instead of English as many of them had done. The result of these changes has been that instead of our traditionally sincere early morning greeting of *"Buenos Días, le dé Diós, Papa"* (Good morning father, God grant you a good day), we get a casual, if not indifferent "Hi, grandpa."

This inability to communicate meaningfully with the elders began to erode the transmission of family values from earlier generations. It was our elders who had transferred their accumulated wisdom, their knowledge and our shared history as we were growing up. There were many of us who remained bilingual but not without great effort on our part. It had simply become easier to become monolingual English speakers in spite of the great loss of connection with our beloved grandparents or great-grandparents who wanted to convey to us the wisdom they had accumulated in their long lives.

This is a loss I personally chose not to endure, given my elders' incredible sacrifices and love and care on behalf of my own generation. These elderly people had been the source of a heritage that I value above all else in my life and I wanted to learn from them what they considered important to pass down to me. Later I would also learn the importance of being multilingual and about the advantages and opportunities available to those who can function in more than one language.

Among other vital changes in life style that we can look back on with regret is the loss of our survival skills. These are skills that had been handed down from one generation to the next, which had allowed us to remain independent. Again, prior to World War II, we had been an agrarian society. When people chose to become more modern, we in effect became part of the industrialize world. This change resulted in a completely different life style. We bought trucks instead of using horse-drawn wagons. We also used tractors to till and plant our fields. We even bought mother an electric washing machine and perhaps even a radio.

As a consequence of our modernization, we began to see a real change in our work ethic. Our values were now in a state of transition. The changes were so subtle that almost without knowing it; our values had become economically centered instead of family centered. Everyone wanted to be paid in money instead of working communally and sharing the benefits as we had done before the war. Furthermore, because of the migration caused by the war, there were fewer able-bodied males around to work.

As fewer people were willing or able to work the land, our attachment began to change concerning what had been our most valuable asset. There were fewer people who truly understood how to care for their land, their crops or their livestock. If the land could not be sold, many simply abandoned their share of the family property saying, "*¿Para que quiero este chamisal? No sirve para nada.*" (Why would I want this pile of worthless sagebrush? It is of no use to me.) In so doing, we lost the ability to feed ourselves, in spite of the fact that we could now get better equipment. We also lost our knowledge of the use of native plants such as wild spinach, purslane, wild onions, berries and piñon. These plants, among others, had supplemented our crops of corn, peas, beans and our summer garden vegetables. The use of native plants both for food and for medicine were simply abandoned and looked down on as inferior to what could be bought at the store.

As we lost our connection to the land and its resources, we lost our ability to provide for ourselves. Thus, instead of having *atole* (cornmeal mush) we bought Cream of Wheat. With the cream of wheat, we bought milk from Creamland Dairy. Milking a cow, even if the family had one to milk was too much trouble. Besides, the kids would not drink the milk because "it comes from the bottom of a cow!" This is what one of my city cousins said after she had been out watching my father milk our cow. Having seen this elsewhere, some city kids gave up drinking milk entirely.

Our livestock, which once had been our major source of grass-fed meat, milk, hides and wool, are only a memory in most people's lives. Given the many restrictions on grazing, the big flocks of sheep were the first to go. Some people kept a few goats which can be grazed close to the house but there are not even very many of those left. Our cattle and horses were once essential to the way we lived. Now they have become such a challenge to keep fed through the winter they are decreasing in number. The summer mountain pasturing of cattle has become such a constant conflict between cattle growers, government agencies and other forest users that many of the cattle growers have simply given up and sold their stock.

Those who continue to raise cattle face further problems. As with some of the other labor-intensive practices, there is now no dependable help to do ranch work. Having seen how much work is involved, younger people moved off to cities and are not available to help. No one can run a cattle or sheep operation single-handedly. There is simply too much hard work involved. My beloved *tía* Maria Aragon used to say when I complained to her that I could not find a good worker, *"Al trabajo y a la guerra, todo el que puede le jerra."* (When it comes to work or war, everyone who is able will avoid it.)

As we continue to tolerate the effects of climate change with insufficient winter snow and drier, hotter summers, we as a community will need to be more creative and conservative about our most precious resource: WATER. We are fortunate to have had good models in the ways our ingenious ancestors used water to benefit us all. At its origin, wetlands and natural ponds and lakes made up most of modern-day Cuba. As these started to dry up, our ancestors began to look for alternatives so they could survive. They developed our *acequia* (irrigation ditch) systems and associations. They built check dams on streams and catch ponds on their properties to utilize the natural flows. They also located as many springs as they could find and marked their locations.

While I was still teaching at Cuba Middle School in the 1990s, I addressed the issue of survival skills with a class of eighth graders. I presented the class with the following question: Among the people you know, who would you choose to be with you in a crisis where your survival was at stake? Given their age (fourteen or fifteen years old) and their lack of crisis experience, they could not think of anyone beyond their own cohort groups. The next question I asked was what skill set each of the people they had selected possessed that would allow them to survive. The students were unable to appreciate the importance of experience as a skill or an advantage in a crisis.

They in turn asked me who I would want with me in a similar situation. I identified the great-grandmother of one of the students. The class was shocked to hear that I would want such an "old fashioned" person to help me. My response to their objections was that I had a great deal to learn about survival from this elderly, gentle, friendly, caring person who had lived the major part of her life in one of the remote ranches near town. She had raised a family on the ranch, grew a wonderful garden and made very infrequent trips into town for supplies.

Perhaps we can still plant a small garden to test our survival skills and supplement the food we buy from stores. If we can get some children to help us, maybe we can show them which end of an onion set goes in the ground first. Possibly we can get them to understand why you plant some vegetables early in the spring and others later. Perhaps they will add that knowledge to their other survival skills and use it in their own lives.

I wonder if our community connections are still strong enough that we can also work cooperatively as our families did in earlier times in order to sustain our heritage without misfortune. We realize that we have come a long way from our self-subsistent pre-war society. However, we are losing our connection to the land, our lifestyle, our language, our culture and our sense of community.

We have learned to accept our dependency on our sometimes irritating and frustrating electronic gadgets. We have even learned to eat foods our great-grandparents would not have recognized, mostly because they are not real. However, this beautiful place which we call home still provides us with some family, loyal friends and neighbors we can depend on to help us survive and perhaps flourish. To this extent, we still enjoy the benefits of the community that it has always been.

Una Plática Sobre una Reunión con el Pasado en San José
(A Conversation About a Reunion with the Past in San José)

San José? Readers might already be asking, which San José? Where? These are valid questions since according to *The Place Names of New Mexico*, by Robert Julyan, San José appears thirty-three times as a New Mexico place name. We know San José is the Spanish version of Saint Joseph, making it a likely name for Hispanic villages. The San José in this chapter, interestingly enough, no longer exists. On the other hand, it would be more accurate to say that reminders of the settlement still persist and only the community no longer exists. Some of the descendants of the people who once occupied this settlement between Cuba and Regina are still part of our communities. As evidence that the village of San José was a significant part of our landscape at one time, we have San José Trail off highway 96 going well up into the mountains east of Regina. Keep in mind that back when there was a San José, the roads to Gallina, Capulín and other settlements were located near the base of the mountains and not where the highway is now.

We also have San José Creek, which meanders from its headwaters between Regina and Llaves down to Cubita, where it drains into the Rio Puerco. Off Highway 96, east of the Regina Post Office, we also have San José Spring, while to the west, on Jicarilla tribal land, there are the San José Lakes. These were resources settlers would have needed for survival and prosperity. It is not surprising that a village would be located near these sources of water and forested land or that it might bear the name of San José.

Again, according to author Robert Julyan, New Mexico place names are not unlike autobiographies of the inhabitants that came before us. Often anonymous and frequently forgotten, these people left behind their language, their relationship to the land, clues about their faith, their struggles and often their tragedies.

In this case, we are left with the reminder that there was once a community of San José in our area. We also have the newer settlement known as Regina. According to Mr. Alexander Schultz, a long-time resident of the area, Regina and San José were not really separate places but parts of a single, emerging settlement. At some point, three gentlemen who settled there petitioned the government for a post office and wrote down San José as the place name. According to local folklore, the U.S. Postal Service rejected their petition because there were already San José post offices elsewhere in the state and that they would have to submit another name. Thus, in 1911, Mr. J. H. Haleri, Mr. W. F. Fish and a Mr. Collier got their post office, which they named after the city of Regina in Saskatchewan, Canada.

We have also learned from a Presbyterian Church register that San José was located twelve miles south of Capulín, near present-day Gallina. This was the location noted by the people who organized and built their first church there. This tells us that at least some neighbors of ours were Spanish-speaking Presbyterian farmers who settled near a dependable source of water for their households and livestock and possibly irrigation.

My quest for San José began several years ago when a leader of Cuba's Presbyterian Church, Mr. Larry Gore, was doing some "domestic archaeology" at the church. While at this task, Mr. Gore came across a church register that he studied briefly and concluded it was not related to Cuba's church since it was labeled San José Church Record. Mr. Gore then entrusted the register to me to see if I could figure out where this treasure came from.

It was through diligent and tedious study of this battered, one-hundred-year-old "San José's Spanish Church Record" that I first became aware of our neighboring, now extinct, village. Through further investigation, more information about the location of San José came to light. Also, an unexpected and precious family history emerged from the brittle old pages, which was by far the most exciting and rewarding part of my quest.

As I delved into this twenty-page, hand-written register, the first thing that struck me was that, with the exception of the minister's name, Reverend Juan C. Quintana, there was not a single name I recognized. What puzzled me even more was that the original thirteen founding members of the church being organized in San José had been "members in good standing" of the Capulín Presbyterian Church. Having read the Capulín Church Register many times, I had discovered that those people were all my relatives. I am a direct descendant of the founding members of that congregation, yet I could not recognize a single name among those original founders of the San José church. I continued to read every page of the minutes of each session meeting, only to find the same names appearing repeatedly as elders or clerks of the session with the same Reverend Quintana as their moderator.

Presbyterian Church Registers are very formulaic in structure and thus very repetitious to read. When researching such old handwritten documents, one hopes for good penmanship and a consistently good pen, which fortunately was the case with this document.

In my desperate effort to try to find a name I recognized, I kept going back to the baptismal records, which started in July 1915. In this record, the first child listed as being baptized at the San José church was a baby girl by the name of Francisquita Padilla. Still I got no clues. I went back to the minutes of the session of that time and discovered that Francisquita was the baby daughter of Mr. Perfeto Padilla, one of the church leaders, and Mrs. Elena Maestas Padilla. Still I had no clue as to who these people were.

As I tried to "connect the dots" related to the inhabitants of San José, I realized that those babies being baptized were of my parents' generation. Their parents would be at least two generations younger than the people who had organized the Capulín church back in 1886.

"Shazam!" as the old comic book saying goes. Baby Francisquita and my mother were direct contemporaries. They were both born in 1915 and coincidently had been the first babies baptized in their respective, newly-built churches. I knew my mother had a friend named Francisquita who lived in La Jara whom I knew casually through sources other than my mother.

As it turned out, I feel the events that followed fall in the category local people call, "This could only happen in Cuba." Why? Because so many of us have known each other for generations and know more or less where we all fit among our respective families and locales.

Not long after I had been pondering who baby Francisquita might have been I found myself at a funeral service sitting right behind my dear friend, Rosita Lopez. I knew her mother's name had been Francisquita and that she was my mother's friend. As we sadly filed out of the church, I managed to whisper to Rosita, asking her if her mother's maiden name had been Padilla. She said yes. I did not see her again except very briefly when I asked her if her grandfather's name had been Perfeto Padilla. Again, she said, "Yes, why?" As we parted to go our separate ways, I was only able to tell her that I thought I had something related to her family that she might be interested in seeing.

It was several days before Rosita and I were able to talk again. I explained to her what I had been given and read off the names of those original founders of the San José church. It turned out that those people were her mother's entire family. She then told me that due to the fact that Doña Francisquita's father (Perfeto Padilla) had died at a very early age they had grown up not knowing much about that part of the family. She thought it was wonderful that she now had this information because in two weeks they were having a family reunion in La Jara. Rosita and her sons worked feverishly making copies of the San José church records to share with their cousins who were coming from Utah, California, Colorado and elsewhere for the reunion.

Later I heard the reunion had been a huge success. Rosita estimated there were between 200 and 250 people who attended and were able to reunite with their relatives and their history. On the Sunday of the reunion, the families met at the old homestead where the grandparents' house is still standing. There at the homestead, they had a worship service that they dedicated to the discovery of their lost family history. Unexpectedly, the old register certainly confirmed their history, faithfully guarded from July 1913 until the church closed. Copies of the document can now be passed down to the generations that follow to show that these were the pioneers and founding families of San José.

Younger people at this gathering would have had little knowledge or appreciation of their San José history. Their families would have moved out in the 1920s looking for jobs or other economic opportunities elsewhere.

This information coincides with the last entry in the church register which is dated April, 1927.

New Mexico still has at least thirty-three other places named San José but only one Regina. Our San José still exists in the ancient register of the "Spanish Presbyterian Church," in the names of creeks and trails and in the memories of those whose families were a part of this now absent community.

Rosita Duran Lopez and Doña Francisquita Padilla Duran, in Doña Francisquita's kitchen in La Jara, New Mexico, circa 1997. Courtesy of Rosita Duran Lopez.

Una Plática Sobre los Libros de Oración
(Conversation about Books of Devotion and Prayer)

This *Plática* is the product of a collection of prayer books and books of religious instruction and devotion, most of which are in Spanish and some of which I was fortunate to inherit. Following the death of my book-loving aunt Josephine DeLaO Lucero in 2001, her children generously offered me a small collection of Catholic prayer books that had belonged to various members of our family during the past three generations. My aunt had amassed these books over many years and after her death, they were distributed among those of us who were interested in such relics.

Among the books I inherited were prayer books that had belonged to my grandfather Eduardo DeLaO, which were worn and tattered from years of carrying them in his shirt pocket during his many sheep herding days far from his home, family and church. There is also a threadbare prayer book that had belonged to my great-great-aunt Lazara Vigil Aragon. This book has the following inscription pasted on the back cover that states in Spanish, in Tia (aunt) Lazara's own hand writing, "This book, *Nuestra Senora de Talpa*, I leave to Josefina Lucero from her aunt Lazara."

Over many years, I have added other equally valuable treasures from other members of the family to my collection. This collection consists of books which people gave me or that I had found abandoned in various places. Some of these books probably began to appear in Cuba with the coming of itinerant priests in the early twentieth century. Together these books have become a useful historical resource as well as a personal link to my family's religious past.

Another source of inspiration that gave rise to this conversation came from a couple of questions I asked one of my many cousins who grew up with me here in Cuba. These are questions I have contemplated over the years as I worked with and observed many modern children and young adults. As I watched, I reflected upon the differences between today's children and my cousins, our friends and me as we were growing up. While engaged in friendly discourse with this cousin and his wife I asked, "why were we (generationally speaking) such good children? Why were we so well behaved?" This, of course, was in comparison to what seems to be going on today among our own children and young people around us. Thus, my pursuit began to answer my own questions. These questions ultimately led me to the treasure trove of books of prayers and devotions. Among the things I found was that many of these books really contained the parameters or boundaries of my generation's behavior as well as those for previous generations living in Northern New Mexico.

As I continued to read these books, I realized that among the facts I wanted in order to answer my questions were the sources and the histories of these books that seemed to have had such a lasting impact on the socialization of several generations of rural people. In particular, I wanted to know how these books had become such an integral part of the lives of people in our rural hamlets. For instance, I recall as a child that among our Catholic population here in Cuba, it seemed that everyone used to take a prayer book and a rosary to church every time they attended Mass. Today people attending a Catholic Mass rarely carry a prayer book. This is one of the major changes I have observed and wondered about.

Another thing that puzzled me as I delved further into my collection is that so many people of my grandparent's generation were virtually uneducated and barely literate. What were the reasons these books were so important to them? I considered the possibility that perhaps literacy was not the issue. Perhaps what was important in bringing up well-behaved and obedient children was that as they were growing up, they would be able to participate in the rituals of their religion as was expected of them by their community.

I know that my maternal grandmother was illiterate, as was her mother. Yet, both my grandmother, Genara DeLaO and my great-grandmother, Petra Vigil CdeBaca knew all the prayers and prayed devoutly throughout their lives. Given these observations, I have to assume that this catalog of prayers had been taught to them from an early age through oral tradition. Having memorized the prayers, they in turn passed them

down to the next generation along with the importance of the devotion
and rituals associated with prayer. The area that is now Cuba was settled
more than a century before it was served even by itinerant priests. During
that time, people gathered around a special area in their homes, decorated
with objects of veneration and devotion to offer their prayers. Only a few
families in this area still have such home altars today.

My mother, Eursina DeLaO Cordova used to recall that her grandmother, Petra Vigil CdeBaca, who could neither read nor write, had taught
her and the other children in the household how to pray. According to
my mother, grandma Petra did this while she supervised and helped the
children go about their daily tasks and chores. As well, my mother recalled
that her grandmother would also gently admonish the children to pray in
a quiet place after their tasks and chores were finished. This tradition continued through my own early childhood. It was at my maternal grandparents' home that I learned how pray in Spanish. Frequently, we all prayed
on our knees at grandmother's home altar. I also recall that by then several
of these prayer books were around other people's homes, including at my
grandparents.

By then my mother and her younger sisters were well able to read.
However, I do not remember that the prayer books were used at home.
Prayers during these periods of devotion were all recited from memory as
were the prayers recited before and after every meal. So again, why were
these prayer books so important? Furthermore, where did these books
come from? People here simply did not have the means to purchase books
of the quality or intellectual level of these books.

I found that several of the books in my collection were published
in Europe or in Mexico in the early twentieth century. For instance, one
of my grandfather's tattered books was published in Switzerland in 1913.
Another one was published in Czechoslovakia in 1906. There is also one
with a beautiful metaphoric title *Ramilletes de Divinas Flores*(A Bouquet of
Divine Flowers), published in Braine-Conte, Belgica (Belgium). This book
contains unusual black on white images accompanying stories related to
the Virgin Mary. Most of these illustrations have the Virgin Mary inside
of a flower. One drawing shows the Virgin inside a giant tulip-like flower

with a caption that reads, "Our Lady in Her Presentation," shown below. I suppose these illustrations are in accord with the general theme of the title of the book. However, this book was not meant for a poorly educated rural farmer or shepherd. In my opinion, this book was intended for a religious scholar. Given the unusual illustrations, I would venture to guess that the scholar this book was meant for would very likely have been European. As well, there is a 1925 revised copy of a book that might have come from Mexico City. However, this book was published by "Franco American Publishing Firm" whose headquarters were in Paris. Given the dates of publication and places where these books were published, nineteenth-century religious scholars and clergy would have written them. These writers would very likely have had eighteenth- and early nineteenth-century educations and an equivalent code of ethics. This code of ethics would have become evident in their writings, including the prayer books in my collection.

Illustration from *Ramillette de Divina Flores*, "Nuestra Señora en su Presentación."

The dates of publication of several books correspond with dates in local Catholic Church documents telling us when priests first came to the Rio Puerco area. According to these documents, itinerant priests were dispatched from Jemez Pueblo to minister in Cuba and other nearby hamlets around 1906. Nevertheless, it was not until 1911–1912 that priests and at least two Franciscan Brothers came as resident clergy to Cuba. We know from an early photograph labeled" Nacimiento Church "and dated 1910 that Cuba had a church but no priests in residence. This first church provided a place of worship only when priests occasionally visited this community. The priests and brothers that came in 1912 began construction of what we call our 1915 church and began building the Convent School. It is my feeling that some of the prayer books in my collection were distributed by these early priests. Throughout these rural areas having books was a luxury. It is also very likely that the books would have been blessed, inscribed by a cleric and given to people as gifts. The local people would have thought these books contained sacred religious wisdom that they felt obliged to follow. These few books along with constant reminding from the clergy became the sources of our common values and code of ethics.

Well into the twentieth century, praying as a family was a common practice that local people observed conscientiously. The rituals included everything from saying grace before and after every meal, before bedtime as well as the first thing in the morning. Most of these books contain bedtime prayers as well as prayers while going to sleep. Some of us remember when more praying was required of all family members during World War II. It was said these prayers were for the safe return of our relatives in the military. We were also "hard-wired" to pray more during family crises such as prolonged illness or a financial emergency, which around here were very common events.

In further studying of the content of the books that people likely took to church, I found that they are very formulaic in composition. There is one titled Id A Jesus: Librito Piadoso para la Buena Niñéz (Go to Jesus: By Way of This Little Book for a Good Childhood). This book and others like it have all the prayers everyone was expected to memorize before First Holy Communion. This book and several others have the complete order of the

Latin Mass with illustrations and explanations of what the priest is doing during each phase of the mass. Thus, the parishioner could follow each step of the Mass. Similarly, these books have the order for the Stations of the Cross with illustrations and the prayers associated with each of the fourteen stations.

In addition to the illustrated order of the Latin Mass and the Stations of the Cross there are specific instructions on how to prepare to go to confession "in a way that would be of greatest benefit". According to the book printed in Czechoslovakia, once the parishioner is in the Confessional Booth he or she could be examined on how or how often the person deviated from each of the Ten Commandments. It seems to me that this rigorous type of examination would, in itself, deter most people from behaving in a manner that could be interpreted by the Father Confessor as a violation of one or more of the Ten Commandments. This presumption begins to shed light on one of my original questions. The reason children and people in general were so well behaved and obedient could well be the threat and fear of having to go to confession. They would have to admit to the Confessor that their actions and behavior had been irresponsible and in violation of church dogma. Following confession, penance would have been assigned. Penance varied from having to say a few prayers before leaving the church to having to attend services for an extended period of time.

Some readers may recall that there was a time when a Catholic in good standing was denied Holy Communion unless he or she had been to confession a short time before. Locally, people used to line up at the Church every Saturday afternoon to go to confession so they could receive Holy Communion at Sunday morning Mass. Until the mid-twentieth century, Catholics in Cuba did not receive communion unless they were fasting. Keep in mind that these rules did not change until after John XXIII became Pope in 1958.

In 1959, the elderly Pope John announced that he would be calling the first Ecumenical Council since 1871. It actually took until 1962 for the Pope to succeed in convening the now famous Second Vatican Council, which lasted until 1965. Unfortunately, Pope John XXIII died in 1963, before the Council ended. He had been Pope for only five years. Following the Second Vatican Council the Roman Catholic Church changed radically in many of its practices. Many of my antiquated prayer books and books of devotion, which meant to instruct parishioners' behaviors, no longer apply as religious dogma today.

Earlier I stated that most of the prayers recited in people's homes were memorized and recited without the aid of a prayer book. There was one exception and that was when a small group of people committed themselves to praying a *Novena*. As the name implies, a *Novena* was prayed for nine days and would be dedicated to a special Saint with recitation of formulaic prayers of devotion for each of the nine days. These prayers were read as prescribed by the *Novena*. Usually those who prayed these *Novenas* were seeking some special favor from the Saint the *Novena* was dedicated to. Among the most popular Novenas practiced here in Cuba were to the *Santo Niño de Atocha*.

The folklore related to the kinds of miracles this Child Saint performed makes it easy to understand his appeal to the rural population of Northern New Mexico. He is believed to have dedicated himself to intervening in behalf of those living in poverty, the disabled and victims of misfortune in general. It also helps to explain why the *Santuario* (The holy shrine) *del Santo Nino de Atocha* in Chimayo, New Mexico, attracts so many visitors in need of solace. During Holy Week, thousands of pilgrims walk from many places all over New Mexico to pay homage to the Child Saint in Chimayo.

After reading and reviewing my collection of prayer books it is my feeling that among the religious books that had the greatest impact on shaping the social behaviors of the community of Cuba were the early Catechisms. These books were used continuously from early childhood until young adulthood. A copy of *Catechism for Beginners*, published in 1930, was the first book in a series of four. Upon reading through the sixty-three pages of *Catechism for Beginners*, which was meant for children in first and second grades, I concluded that herein exists the answer to my second question about why the children of my generation and of children before us were such good and obedient kids. Given that first and second graders are between five and eight years of age and were being drilled on the content of this book I am certain we would have become very good and obedient children. Part one of the little book contains all the prayers the children were expected to memorize before they were eligible for First Holy Communion. These prayers go beyond simple morning, evening and mealtime prayers. These are prayers such as the Apostles' Creed, Prayers for Confession, as well as an Act of Contrition. This material seems to me to be a heavy psychological burden of guilt and fear to bear at such a young age, even for an eight-year-old.

The second part of this *Catechism for Beginners* consists of seventy-three questions with answers that must be memorized. Question #16, which is set out for these very young children reads: "What will happen to bad people who do not love and serve God?" Answer: "Bad people, who do not love and serve God, will be punished with hell-fire." Question #18 "What is sin?" Answer: "Sin is any willful thought, word, deed, or omission contrary to the law of God." There is also a series of questions following the Ten Commandments that directly relate to human behaviors which are the foundation of the good, well behaved and obedient childhood some of us remember. Question #59 which follows the Ten Commandments and the precepts of the Church reads: "What are some of the sins committed against the Ten Commandments?" There are eight answers to this question, which as you may recall were meant for children five to eight years old. Among these answers are: "Not to say our prayers (morning, night, and table prayers), Not to study our catechism. To believe in dreams, fortune-tellers omens and charms. To be angry. To look at, think or speak of immodest things. To do immodest things alone or with others". According to the introduction to *Catechism for Beginners*, the book that follows in this series is intended for use in the lower grades and contains the Latin prayers for alter boys. The group from which altar boys were selected used this volume and those boys would have been expected to memorize these prayers in Latin.

To my knowledge, these Catechism books were distributed by the local Catholic Church without charge to the students or the parents. By 1930, the local Convent School had been in full operation for ten years and staffed by as many as twelve Franciscan nuns. Catechism and daily mass were part of the schedule. The Church next door to the Convent also had no fewer than two priests in residence and they were available to support all religious education efforts at all times.

According to the Convent School archives, during the school year 1932-1933, the school had been accredited to teach High School, which would allow for an increase in enrollment. There were thirty students enrolled for High School along with the entire enrollment in the lower grades, which comprised 246 students in grades one through eight. The 246 students would be taking Catechism classes every day as well as their other scheduled classes. In addition to the students that were enrolled in the Convent School, Catechism was also taught in the hamlets outside of Cuba, such as La Jara and San Luis. During the decades of Convent School religious education, there were years when First Holy Communion classes could exceed twenty to thirty children who had become eligible for this event by passing the rigors of the Catechism books such as the one I reviewed.

Earlier, I presented the question of what kind of impact these books of prayer, devotion and religious instruction might have had on communities such as Cuba. I have concluded that many of these books actually laid out the fundamental rules of behavior for several generations of people in rural Northern New Mexico. I also believe that in communities where there was little or no other source of information, such as newspapers, magazines or radio, people who could read relied on these books for inspiration and to guide their belief systems. Since there were no other sources of information that would have conflicted with these books, most people never questioned the authority of their churches nor did they recognize it as a form of indoctrination of a very narrow scope.

Again, keep in mind that it was not until after World War II that life in Northern New Mexico began to change. Many of the changes that occurred were due mainly to the fact that so many people had been to other places and had seen how other people lived and did things differently from our archaic ways.

As for the Roman Catholic Church, it was not until the Second Vatican Council of 1962 that real changes from some of the things I have found in these ancient books really occurred. Those changes brought about the practices of the Church as it is today. Liberal as the changes might seem to some more traditional and conservative followers, the Catholic Church seems a far more amicable institution today than what it was before 1962.

Books of prayers and religious instruction such as those in my collection still hold literary, cultural and educational value. As for those of us who knew and loved the people who truly treasured these books there is tremendous sentimental attachment to these books despite their tattered and worn conditions. In reviewing these resources, we can better understand what the forces were that changed our social behaviors from what we knew to be correct to what we have today. Another value these books hold is that we can gain a deeper appreciation how and why our children and their children behave differently from us. Whether or not we agree with the current modes of behaviors is irrelevant, what is important is to know how we got to where we are today.

First Holy Communion, Father Leonard with thirty-five communicants, circa 1935.

First Holy Communion, Father Leonard with twenty-five communicants, circa 1939.

Father Leo, one of the Cuba Convent Sisters, a lay teacher and twenty-four communicants,
La Jara; no date. Courtesy of Florence Garcia Martinez.

Rosie DeLaO and first cousin Eloy Aragon on First Holy Communion day, circa 1941.

Una Plática de Costumbre Devota
(A Conversation about a Labor of Love and Devotion)

We here in Cuba had a little-known community treasure that resulted from a labor of love, devotion and heartfelt memories of our beloved 1915 Immaculate Conception Church.

The two people responsible for providing our community with this historical prize are Mr. Fidencio Aragon and his loyal partner and wife Julia Chavez Aragon. Together they spent nearly four years building a near replica of the interior and exterior of the Cuba Catholic Church, which was completed in 1915. This church had not only been the center of religious activity, it was the heart and soul of each of its members from their first blessing at baptism to their final benediction at the *campo santo* (cemetery). In the early 1960s, the church was declared structurally unsafe due to settling of the building resulting from snow collecting on the north side of the structure during its many winters. In February 1965, the church was razed to the ground, much to the sorrow and sense of enormous loss of the entire community. The ground was leveled and preparations for the building of the new church began immediately.

As the Spanish title of this article indicates, there is in northern New Mexico a *costumbre* (tradition) of crafting religious or devotional items for reasons of great love and passion. Among the best known of these are the *Santos* (woodcarvings in the round of Saints). There are also *retablos* (paintings of religious subjects on flat surfaces, usually wooden planks or boards). As well, there is a custom of building small facsimiles of churches. These are frequently built as offerings to a patron saint such as the *Santo Niño* at the famous *Santuario del Santo Niño de Atocha* (The shrine of the Holy Child of Atocha) in Chimayo, New Mexico.

Many of these church replicas are quite small and rustic in workmanship. The two examples seen in Photograph 10 were apparently taken to the *Santuario* and left on the courtyard wall as offerings.

What differentiates the Aragones' labor of love from others I have seen is the huge size of the structure. The impeccable attention and the quality of workmanship that Mr. and Mrs. Aragon put into this enormous treasure are obvious in Photograph 11.

In an interview with Mrs. Aragon, I asked her what the motivation had been for the building of this detailed replica of Cuba's 1915 church. Mrs. Aragon related to me that several years before they built their church she had been to visit a friend whose husband had built a miniature reproduction of a church. She admired that reproduction very much and when she returned from her visit, she related to her husband the details of their friends' church and how impressed she had been by the work.

Eventually, both Mr. and Mrs. Aragon went to visit these acquaintances together and Mr. Aragon also got to see the model church. On the way home, Mr. Aragon told his wife that he was going to build a replica of the old church in Cuba. Mrs. Aragon was taken by the idea and responded positively to such a project.

After all, this was the church where their wedding had taken place in November of 1957 and it held many family and childhood memories for both of them. Mrs. Aragon said she did not give the project much thought after that trip but a short time later she did notice that her husband was starting to collect what seemed like small building materials. She also said that once Mr. Aragon asked if they had a picture of the old church, she knew then that they were committed to a major project. What neither of them realized at the time was that it would take nearly three years of evenings while watching television and many weekends to complete their church to the level of perfection they both wanted. For one thing, they only had a few photographs of the church and each other's recollections of what the church had looked like.

Photograph 12 is an early 1930s picture and among the oldest pictures I have of the 1915 church. I chose to include it here instead of a later photograph in order to explain an interesting feature in the Aragon church that is not shown in this picture but is prominent in later photographs. Notice that in the early 1930s picture there is no statue of the Virgin Mary in what used to be a window above the round window over the main entrance to the church. According to the chronicles of the Cuba Convent School, an entry dated February 5, 1946, states, "In thanksgiving for the safe return of the soldiers who served in World War II, a statue of the Blessed Virgin was blessed and placed in a niche in the tower of the church." A statue of the Blessed Virgin is very visible in the Aragon church and in all photographs of the church taken after 1946.

From what Mrs. Aragon recalls, apparently her husband had drawn the plans for their church to the scale and size he had visualized the finished project to look like. He apparently had also planned how to proceed with the construction of the interior as well as the exterior features that he wanted to focus on. Some of these features were constructed to allow the viewers to appreciate the builders' labor and devotion to detail inside the church as well as outside.

The building is set on a four- by six-foot platform and from the platform to the top of the cross on the steeple it measures four feet, two inches in height. The entire exterior of the structure is carefully stuccoed and painted. The wood is all sanded, stained and varnished. The doors all open and close on their tiny hinges. The windows all have glass panels and the metal roof is flawlessly finished. The central part of the roof can be removed to allow viewing of the entire interior of the church. Note also, the tiny electrical light fixtures at the corners of the roof in the front of the building in Photograph 11. This is a feature the original church lacked that would have been greatly appreciated in its time. Mr. Aragon provided his church with electric lights so that it can be examined at night as well as in the daytime.

Unfortunately, photographs of the interior do not allow the reader to appreciate the amazing detail and skilled workmanship that Mr. and Mrs. Aragon devoted to this work of art. The altars are meticulously crafted, painted white and trimmed with gold paint. The statues of the saints are respectfully placed in their niches, as is a small lamb peacefully at rest at the bottom of the main altar. Mrs. Aragon stated that finding statues of the saints in the appropriate size had been a real challenge in completing the project.

The wood throughout the interior of the structure is also sanded, stained and varnished. Each tiny pew was individually made and its kneeling bench attached so that they can be lowered or raised as they are in real churches. There must be at least twelve of these pews on either side of the church, each with its attached kneeling bench. As well, the communion rail has a little gate that opens and closes as it did in the real church.

For those of you who have been lucky enough to enjoy and admire this marvelous piece of folk art when it was on display at Cuba Fiestas on at least two occasions understand what I have been trying to describe. The Aragones are now very reluctant to move the model because during both of its previous moves the structure suffered minor damage. Currently Mr. and Mrs. Aragon have stored this labor of love and devotion in a porch they closed in at one of their houses to keep it safe.

I first became aware of this remarkable treasure in early 2012. Since then, I have made inquiries at several places where this piece of work can be appreciated by more people while keeping it safe from destruction or damage. Like Mrs. Aragon, who has also been looking for a permanent home for their church, we have been unable to find a museum, a school or a municipality that wants to assume responsibility for our local treasure.

Personally, I thought the Aragon church belongs in Cuba. I also believe it would be an interesting artistic attraction as well as a solemn reminder of the void left in the lives of people who had loved our ancient church.

Some months later, following the original article in the *Cuba News*, word came to me that a new and wonderful home had been found for the Cuba Church replica built by Mr. and Mrs. Aragon. What follows is a story within a story with very positive results.

As I understand the chain of events, the City of Belen acquired what used to be the once-famous Fred Harvey Restaurant facility at the Belen Railroad Station to develop into a local museum. It is now known as the Harvey House Museum of Belen.

What happened next is truly amazing. Mr. and Mrs. Aragon have twin great-granddaughters who were taken on a school field trip to the new museum. There these thirteen-year-old girls were shown some church replicas of the sort I mentioned earlier. These replicas are apparently small and some are better crafted than others but all are basically small pieces of devotional folk art. The girls looked at what was on display and mentioned to someone on the staff that their great-grandpa Fidencio had built a replica of Cuba's Immaculate Conception Church that was bigger and far more detailed than what was on display. Apparently, they also mentioned that the story of their great-grandpa's church had been in the Cuba newspaper.

Within a few days, the family was contacted by the museum and Debbie Tafoya, Mr. and Mrs. Aragon's daughter, took her copy of the *Cuba News* and shared it with the people at the museum. Upon reading the article, one of the gentlemen in charge noted that our Aragon church did not have a home. Mr. Ron Torres then contacted the Aragones and apparently offered them a home for their church. There was a slight problem in that no one in the family would give up their copy of the *Cuba News* article for the museum to use as a source of information for their display. Not long after, Mr. Torres contacted me for a copy of the article which I provided for his use.

A few days later, Mrs. Aragon called me to say that the museum was picking up the church from where it had been stored here in Cuba. We talked about how fortunate it was that her two great-granddaughters, Cheyenne and Cherish were keen enough to speak up and bring attention and appreciation to their great-grandfather's work, resulting in a permanent home for this work of art.

The good news about our Cuba Church does not end with the finding of a home. Later, I received a call from a writer for the *Valencia County Bulletin* who wanted to do a feature article on the Aragon church and its history. Apparently, the church has become a popular attraction in Belen. Perhaps if Cuba had been more proactive in finding an appropriate home here in Cuba, the attraction would be here instead of Belen. In my conversation with Mr. Torres, I assured him I would go to Belen to visit their new museum and to visit our church. Like much of our folk art, we now have to travel elsewhere to see it and so it is with the Aragon church. However, now it will have far more exposure than it would have gotten here.

Once the museum had set up its display, they needed information about the church. Again, Mr. Torres called me for some history of the Cuba Church which could be included in the exhibit. I agreed to provide the museum with the needed information which would be relevant to visitors to the museum. As well. there are now at least two generations of local young people and new families who have moved into our community who never saw our beloved 1915 church and do not know its history or its prominence in our community.

The historical information requested by the museum follows with few revisions as a separate document titled, "A Brief History of Immaculate Conception Church, Cuba, New Mexico, 1914–1965."

Brief History of Immaculate Conception Church, Cuba, New Mexico, 1914–1965

According to the few existing documents related to this Immaculate Conception Church of Cuba, its building was begun in 1911 and completed in 1915.

At the time, Immaculate Conception Parish in Cuba had been under the charge of St. John the Baptist Province of Cincinnati, Ohio since about 1906. This would have been approximately fifty-five years after the now famous arrival of Bishop Jean Baptist Lamy in Santa Fé from Cincinnati in August of 1851. His charge at the time was to head the newly established Bishopric of New Mexico. This ecclesiastical reorganization followed the American conquest of Mexican territory in 1848, including what is now the entire American Southwest. Today, the events that brought about these changes are known as the Mexican-American War, a part of the concept of Manifest Destiny.

Local church records state the two Franciscan priests, a Father Barnabes Meyer and Father Camilus Fangman had made trips to the Cuba area from the Mission in Jemez Pueblo during the early part of the twentieth century to care for the spiritual needs of the people in the Rio Puerco Valley. Given that there was already a church building in Cuba at that time, documented by a photograph of that church dated 1910, it appears that it was Father Camilus' longing for "better facilities" in Cuba, that plans for this particular church began. Hence construction was started in 1911, under the supervision of a Franciscan Brother in residence by the name of Livor. Local people provided the labor force. It is also stated that the chief carpenter was local. Given that this event took place over one hundred years ago, it is not clear who this chief carpenter might have been. Unfortunately, he was not named in the documents. Interestingly, it is documented that the adobes for this church were made and donated by local families. It is also said in the local folklore that this church was "quite an edifice" in its day, given the lack of local resources and the small number of people living here then. This edifice must have been built at tremendous sacrifice by the local parishioners. The walls of the church were made of adobes and it is said that they measured between thirty-two and thirty-six inches thick. Its design was the traditional cruciform and held about three hundred people. When the church was completed in 1915, it was the largest building in Cuba. The only building larger than the church would be the three-story Convent school next door which was not completed until 1921.

Once the adobe walls were dry and all of the cracks were sealed, a rough coat of special mud was slapped onto the adobes by hand but not smoothed out. After this rough coat of mud was dry, the women in the community were ready to begin applying the smooth coat of plaster onto the building. This would have been done by the younger women under the watchful eye of the older, experienced women. The men would help mix the mud, haul the water and the specific kind of clay that was needed to keep the women plastering well supplied with what they required to complete this enormous project.

The interior of this church had a high, cathedral-style ceiling which was made out of tongue-and groove lumber. This high ceiling accommodated a massive, beautiful main alter at the front of the church. As well, there was a large upstairs choir loft in the back of the church. This loft had an organ and room enough for a choir of a dozen or more members to stand comfortably and sing at every mass, rosary, wedding and funeral. The church also had a basement, or perhaps better called a large cellar. The heating system for the church and probably for the attached rectory, which was built later, was located in this underground part of the church.

Over the years, the walls of the church began to push out on the north side, due to the tremendous weight of the walls, ceiling and the corrugated metal roof. Snow coming off the north side of the large roof accumulated over the winter months and the area around and under the church was damp for long periods of time. Some time later pilasters were built along the outside of the north wall and tie-rods were installed inside the church in an effort to stop further damage. Unfortunately, these remedies failed to halt the deterioration of this beloved building.

During the winter of 1964, some preliminary plans were drawn for a new church and rectory. Having gotten the Bishop's permission to raze the whole structure on February 14, 1965, the last masses were sadly heard by generations of faithful parishioners. After fifty years, this church which had been a source of pride, inspiration and comfort to its congregation was closed and completely demolished. To this day, this old church remains in the memories of all those who were fortunate enough to worship peacefully, celebrate the significant events of their lives and quietly weep over their personal losses.

Historically, this Immaculate Conception Church has been one of Cuba's greatest landmarks and sources of local history. Its destruction was one of the community's greatest losses, obviously not yet forgotten.

Immaculate Conception Church, Cuba, New Mexico, early 1930s.

Fidencio and Julia (Chavez) Aragon with their replica of the 1915 Cuba Church. This photograph of Mr. and Mrs. Aragon in front of their church is included in appreciation for their labor of love and devotion to the memory of what was once the heart and soul of the community of Cuba, New Mexico. Photograph by Don Moore.

Una Plática de Felicidades
(A Congratulatory Conversation)

On April 23, 1889, the Presbyterian Church of Nacimiento was organized by Reverend John M. Shields and eleven members of the community of Nacimiento (a part of what is now known as Cuba). In 2014, this church, which was later named the Cuba Spanish Presbyterian Church, celebrated its one hundred twenty-fifth anniversary on Saturday, May 31.

The celebration began at 1:00 p.m. at the church. Invitations were mailed out to many people who had been associated with the church previously and an open invitation was published in the May 20, 2014, issue of the *Cuba News*. Everyone was welcome to attend this informal open house, refreshments and reunion of friends and members alike.

Given the many trials and tribulations this congregation has endured and the successes it has achieved calls for sincere congratulations from the community it has served.

The history of the Cuba Presbyterian Church is essentially the history of a small group of people who, for a century and a quarter, have persisted in keeping the doors of their little church open for themselves as well as for anyone else who cares or needs to join in worship.

According to church documents, the Cuba Church, like the San José Church described in previous chapters is a direct offshoot of the churches in Jemez and Capulín. These churches were organized beginning in 1878 when Reverend Shields arrived in Jemez Pueblo with the specific task of ministering to New Mexico's Native American population. He actually built a church and a school in Jemez Pueblo. This is the only non-Catholic church that has ever been allowed to exist in the Pueblo to this day. From Jemez Pueblo, Reverend Shields expanded his mission to Jemez Springs, where his family and staff lived because non-Pueblo people were not allowed to live on Pueblo land. Apparently not finding much success among the

Pueblo people, Reverend Shields began to focus on Hispanic communities that were more receptive to his brand of ministry.

In March 1887, Reverend Shields helped organize the Capulín church with the help of ordained elders from Jemez Springs. According to the official Capulín register, the original members of that church numbered fourteen, "with nine more expected to join."

As I studied the list of the original fourteen members of the Capulín Church, it appeared that several of those people were related to people who later organized the Nacimiento Church in 1889. The Cuba Church congregation in still comprised primarily of direct descendants of the fourteen original members of the Capulín Church and members of the Jemez Springs Church.

In 1890, again according to church documents, the entire Pasqual Cordova clan asked for letters of transfer from the Capulín Church to the newly established church in Nacimiento. Later in the early 1900s, a group of the Antonio Cordova family also moved to the Nacimiento Church, as did the Paulin Montoya family who transferred from the Jemez Springs Church. Unfortunately, records do not specify whether these people came from the Jemez Springs Church or the Jemez Pueblo Church. It is more likely that they transferred from the Jemez Springs Church since non-Pueblo people were not allowed to live on Pueblo land.

Little is known about the original Nacimiento Church except for its approximate location. During an interview I had with the late Lionel Chavez in March of 2001, he confirmed that the original church was located near the site of the current Presbyterian cemetery located just off Highway 126 on the present-day Southern All-Around Road.

Lionel Chavez was the son of Francisco Antonio Chavez whose family donated the land for the original Nacimiento Church. Lionel said the Chavez family had also donated the land for the cemetery, which is still in use. As well, Mr. Chavez also confirmed that the original church had burned down around 1925–1926. He also recalled hearing in his family lore that following the loss of the church, the congregation met at Don Francisco Chavez's home for services.

The information about the original Nacimiento Church around 1925–1926 coincides with what Emma Eichwald Martinez Sandoval wrote in *Remembering Presbyterian Missions in the Southwest*. Here she wrote about the construction in 1927 of the current Presbyterian Church located on Church Lane in Cuba. This was the period when Emma's husband, Reverend Ubaldo J. Martinez became pastor of Cuba's church the first time.

According to Mrs. Sandoval, Reverend Martinez had just returned to New Mexico from McCormick Seminary in Chicago and Cuba was his first assignment as an ordained minister. Not only was this his first assignment but the National Mission supervisor of ministries in New Mexico informed him that his first duty was to build a new church. The congregation wanted their new church built closer to what was becoming Main Street in Cuba but they did not own any property in town. Church documents and oral history confirm that the land on which the present church was built was donated by Mr. Aron (Don Augustin) Eichwald.

Mrs. Sandoval says in her account that the young Reverend Martinez had not been aware that the Board of National Missions had an architectural department that designed new churches. Thus, Reverend Martinez designed what is now Cuba's present church himself. Reverend Martinez formed a building committee consisting of Lugardo Cordova, his younger brother Julian Cordova, their first cousin Lydia Gutierrez and their good friend and carpenter, Francisco Chavez. They began to make adobes for their new church immediately.

The adobe walls for Reverend Martinez's large rectangular building were completed by the end of the summer of 1927. The building had a basement excavated below the sanctuary but the building had no roof because they had run out of money.

Eventually the supervisor of ministries agreed to provide the money for the roof. By the time the roof was to be constructed, the walls had been left unplastered and unprotected through the winter and had started to bow outward. Now, even though Reverend Martinez had the money for the roof, apparently no one wanted the job of building the roof for fear that the whole structure would collapse.

Lionel Chavez said that his father, Don Francisco Chavez was the one who finally figured out how to bring the walls back into alignment and then agreed to construct the roof without danger of the walls collapsing. Even today, one can see three metal rods that cross the top of the sanctuary that Don Francisco used to straighten the walls. The church was completed in 1929. In July of 1937, new church seats were bought for $7.50 each. Each family member in the congregation was charged fifty cents to pay for the new seats.

Over the years, the church building has gone through many phases of modernization, renovation and, more recently, preservation. Today the building is certainly more comfortable and more useful to its members.

One of the truly unique features of this church is that it is the only church in town that uses a real bell to call its members to worship. Other churches in town either do not have bells or have an electronic bell such as the one on the Catholic Church.

In its one hundred twenty-five years, this church has had approximately twenty different pastors and at least thirteen interim ministers. In spite of the unfavorable stories related to Cuba's climate and its sometimes-inhospitable population, there have been ministers that have lived among us for many years, as can be seen from the list that follows. Reverend Shields, for instance, was minister for a total of twelve years. He was here two different times, serving for six years each time. Reverend Ubaldo J. Martinez also ministered twice. The first time he was here for four years and when he returned in 1945, he served for eleven years. Reverend Juan C. Quintana was here for fourteen years. From some of the reading I have done about Reverend Quintana, he appears to have been controversial in some quarters but generally a very popular and interesting individual among most people. I do recall hearing that he was a photographer and very likely took many of the surviving pictures of Cuba and its citizens during his tenure.

Reverend Wayne Parker, who many readers may recall, was here between 1984 and 1995. He dedicated eleven years of service to this community. A Reverend E. M. Fenton was here from 1895 to 1898. He is most likely the son of the more famous Presbyterian minister and engineer who served at Jemez Pueblo and Jemez Springs. According to Robert Julyan's

Place Names of New Mexico, "The State Park, the lake it features and the old ranch surrounding it were all named for Elijah McClean Fenton, Sr., a Presbyterian minister and civil engineer, who came to New Mexico in 1881 and was stationed at Jemez Pueblo in 1892." There are others such as Reverend Victoriano Valdez, who was here between 1931 and 1940. His descendants are still among us. He is personally special to me because during his nine-year tenure he baptized those of us born in the 1930s that are now about 80 years of age or older.

In closing, I would like to recount a short story written by the Mexican author Juan Rulfo. I believe this story relates to the history I have shared in this chapter. Rulfo's story is titled *Luvinia.* Luvinia is a hamlet not unlike Cuba, located on some desolate mountain, which is almost impossible to reach.

In the story, a visitor is trying to reach Luvinia and when he finally arrives, he finds the place almost uninhabitable. The constant winds, dust and probably weeds are unpleasant elements: the same conditions that make some of our own lowland cousins uncomfortable when they come to visit.

When the visitor to Luvinia finally gets out of the wind and into a public eatery, he looks around at the people and asks, "How can you people live in this God-forsaken place? Why don't you leave here?" The people listen to him patiently and finally someone asked the stranger, "And if we left Luvinia, who would take care of our dead?"

This is an important question to ask in a church such as Cuba Presbyterian. Our dead are our history. Remember, earlier I mentioned the cemetery? In that cemetery are buried generations of our ancestors. More importantly, there lie the bones of many of the original eleven members who formed this church in 1889. Those of us here not only continue to take care of our dead but we also take care of the living. We keep the doors of our little Presbyterian Church open for anyone who wishes to worship there.

Ministers

Rev. J.M Shields
Rev. E.M. Fenton
Rev. E.C. Chavez
Rev. J.J. Van Wagner
Rev. C.H. Perea
Rev. J.C. Quintana
Rev. U.J. Martinez
Rev. V. Valdez
Rev. M. Cruz
Rev. G. De Pree
Rev. J. Nash
Rev. W.T. Hoffmeyer
Rev. P. Calhoun
Rev. P. Sanchez
Rev. P. Romero
Rev. F. Link
Rev. T. Spath
Rev. W. Parker
Rev. O.E. Hinnant

Interim Ministers

Rev. Nelson Wright
Rev. Thomas Gonzales
Rev. Alvaro Maestas
Rev. Jaime Quinones
Rev. Horacia Rendon
Rev. Ken Cuthberson

Rev. Daniel Erdman
Rev. William Aber
Rev. H. Freeman Davis
Rev. Joyce Thompson
Rev. Henry Archuleta
Rev. Wilfred Sawyier

List of ministers who served at Cuba Presbyterian Church for one hundred twenty years.

Cuba Presbyterian Church, 1945, when it still had a belfry and chimney.
Courtesy of Menaul Historical Library.

Mrs. Uvaldo Martinez (front row) with young people, Cuba Presbyterian Church,
Easter, circa 1951. Reverend Martinez is in the back, left corner.
Courtesy of Menaul Historical Library.

Last day of Vacation Bible School, circa 1947. Courtesy of Cuba Presbyterian Church.

Una Plática Recordando los Acontecimientos del Pasado
(A Conversation Recalling the Events of the Past)

(Note: this chapter was originally written as a newspaper article in March, 2014, the fiftieth anniversary of the events described below. These events are still worth remembering.)

Twenty-first-century readers may wonder what was so special about 1964. As a twentieth-century person, I can assure you that, as you read this chapter, you will understand what made 1964 a year like no other in the lives of many of us who lived through that year. You may have to go to other sources to find who the Beatles were, what a drill team does or what a "jumper" is. All of this was a part of life in 1964.

Recently, we have been bombarded with television film footage noting the fiftieth anniversary of various events that occurred in 1964. Of these, the one that probably received the greatest attention was the arrival of the Beatles in February of that year and their appearance on the "Ed Sullivan Show" on television. That got me thinking about all the other things that were going on then. Perhaps this is a good time to reminisce about those times and those events.

As a nation, we entered the new year on January 1st, still reeling from the assassination of President John F. Kennedy the previous November. While still stunned, we awaited the results of the Warren Commission's investigative report related to the President's assassination. In spite of human tragedies or natural disasters, the world has a way of moving on and so we did. Now, fifty years later, as we look back on the events of 1964, we clearly define that year as a pivotal period in mid-twentieth-century history.

For those of you who were born in 1964, you are now half a century old (or more): Congratulations! Not unlike Columbus in 1492, you have gotten far more from your "trip" than you might have expected. For those of us who already had a fair amount of experience with the world as it had been, both the range and the speed of change have astounded us since that time. For all of us, the world changed in front of our eyes and would never go back to what it had been before.

In 1964, our country was in a virtual state of social revolution. There were race riots in one major city after another. Parts of some of these cities were burned down as a result of these riots. Yet, amid this chaos of riots and burning cities, we got wonderful news from outer space. Our spacecraft, Ranger 7, started to convey the first pictures of the moon's surface. Since the same side of the moon always faces us, this was the first time in history we were able to see the backside of the moon. According to the *New York Times,* this was considered "the greatest advance in lunar astronomy since Galileo." President Lyndon Johnson hailed this new lunar feat, calling it a "basic step" toward a manned landing on the moon by United States astronauts. That would happen six years later.

At the same time, we were looking forward to American astronauts landing on the moon, the war in Vietnam began to escalate. Again, according *The New York Times,* President Johnson announced to the nation on a national radio and television broadcast that U.S. planes had attacked North Vietnamese bases in retaliation for what was believed to have been attacks on U.S. ships in the Gulf of Tonkin, just off the coast of North Vietnam. What the president called a "limited retaliation" was that the number of troops needed in Vietnam increased dramatically. On the home front, the antiwar movement on major university campuses and in large urban areas sometimes got out of control. There were huge antiwar demonstrations on and off campuses across the country while police in riot gear tried in vain to restrain the demonstrators. At the University of California at Berkeley, for example, the National Guard was called out to help the police. They used helicopters, tear gas and loaded one police van or bus after another with defiant students and normally law-abiding citizens for their protests.

At the same time, either because of being drafted or because of a true sense of responsibility to their country, other young men and women joined the military and served their country in that war, many with great distinction. These individuals did their duty but did not return to a hero's welcome but to a nation deeply divided over their involvement in that war.

Vietnam was seen by many as an extremely unpopular war and may still be considered controversial. Even today, fifty years later, some of the wounds of those who served are still unhealed.

Along with everything else that was going on, 1964 was an election year. Lyndon Johnson, who had completed President Kennedy's term, was running against the Republican candidate Barry Goldwater. Television had first become important in the 1960 election and was a major factor in 1964. The candidates had very different views on most issues; the polls suggested a close race and every vote counted. Political advertising on television became a part of our lives in 1964.

The Civil Rights Act of 1964 had passed, giving voting rights to all citizens. The twenty-fourth amendment to the Constitution had also been ratified in January of 1964, banning the poll tax as a prerequisite for voting in federal elections. Race could no longer be used to prevent people from voting. Incidentally, the passing of this law was accomplished in large measure through the long-term efforts of New Mexico's Senator Dennis Chavez.

As mentioned earlier, in 1964, the nation was in a state of social revolution. The Civil Rights Movement against racial discrimination was getting stronger and those who opposed it were becoming more violent. This Movement, under the leadership of Dr. Martin Luther King, Jr. and the Southern Christian Leadership Conference, committed to nonviolent civil disobedient protest, were trying to get as many Black people eligible to vote as possible in the November election. There were people from all over the country going into the segregated southern states helping Black people register to vote. Unfortunately, many of these activists were beaten and jailed and several were murdered in their efforts to secure the rights for everyone to be able to vote. Ultimately, their efforts did prove successful and had a great impact on the 1964 election. In honor of his efforts to promote nonviolent change, Dr. Martin Luther King, Jr. was awarded the Nobel Peace Prize in 1964.

Political changes elsewhere also had an impact on America in 1964. Premier Nikita Khrushchev was relieved of his political position in that year and was replaced by Leonid Brezhnev. Some of you may remember when Mr. Khrushchev attended a meeting of the United Nations some years earlier and was so adamant in his protest of an American policy, he took off his shoe and banged it on the podium to emphasize his point of view. He received a lot of press by doing this and got the attention of many delegates but had little effect on American policy. From that time on, the USSR gradually decayed and finally fell apart in 1991.

That decay was not obvious in 1964, however. Hungary had failed in its attempt to separate itself from Soviet domination in 1957 and the "Prague Spring" revolt failed to free Czechoslovakia in 1965. Decolonization was in full swing in Africa with many countries already and others at war or yet to begin the move toward independence. Che Guevara had swept from Cuba across parts of Latin America and was probably at the height of his popularity in 1964. Mao Zedong was the only leader modern China had known. His "Great Leap Forward" had led to the starvation of millions before 1964 and his "Cultural Revolution" would send millions from cities into the country to raise more food crops shortly after that. In America, "Duck and Cover" was an exercise to protect children from attack by atomic bombs and was in general practice in schools all across the country through the 1960s. Every city had a public alert system to warn of a possible nuclear attack.

Just prior to the election of 1964, President Johnson made his vision of "The Great Society" known to the nation. This was, in part, his plan for more equality among the poor and disenfranchised if he were reelected.

In September 1964, just before the election, the Warren Commission concluded its investigation into the assassination of President Kennedy. Chief Justice Earl Warren and his fellow commissioners unanimously concluded that Lee Harvey Oswald had acted alone as the assassin and that there was no conspiracy, foreign or domestic. All these years later, there are still people who question the findings and we may never know anything more than what the report said. Doubt about the Warren Commission's report has caused people to look at similar reports from later special commissions with considerable skepticism.

Sports lovers, for whom politics is secondary, may recall that the St. Louis Cardinals beat the favored New York Yankees in the World Series 1964. It was also in that year that Cassius Clay, later known as Muhammad Ali, first won the World Heavyweight boxing championship. The 1964 Olympics were held in Tokyo. The Soviet Union went home with 96 total medals as compared to 90 for the United States. The United States won more Gold Medals than the Soviets and these two teams so dominated the games that together they took home as many medals as the next seven countries combined. "Joltin' Joe" Frazier won the heavyweight gold medal and went on to be one of the greatest boxers of the next several decades. Billy Mills, an Oglala Lakota (Sioux) from Pine Ridge, South Dakota, was another star of that Olympic competition. His struggle to get into the Olympics is chronicled in the film, "Running Brave." He won the gold medal in the 10,000-meter run and also competed in the marathon. I have had students who had actually met Mr. Mills after his Olympic experience when he used to travel to reservations in an effort to inspire young people to become winners at any sport they were passionate about.

The Winter Olympics were also held that year in Innsbruck, Austria. The U.S. did not do so well in that competition. (Summer and winter Olympics were held in the same year until 1968.)

Neither the politics, the war nor the thrill of the sports world would compare with the highlight in the lives of the "Swingers" of 1964. "On February 7, 1964, the Beatles landed in New York, greeted by thousands of screaming fans. Two nights later, 73 million viewers in the United States and millions more in Canada tuned in to watch John, Paul, George and Ringo make their American debut on the Ed Sullivan Show. The British Invasion had begun." This quote is from a Daedalus Books Catalog where they advertise a limited-edition CD version of the Beatles' American Albums. These "mini-LP replicas" are even being packaged in scaled-down copies of the original album covers including their paper liner sleeves. Beatles lovers, now you can have it all. Oh, and try to guess what the most popular song was in 1964. If you guessed "I Want to Hold Your Hand," by the Beatles, you would be right!

The most popular movies of that year reflect the state of transition in the country at that time. "A Hard Day's Night" by the Beatles and the James Bond "Goldfinger" were at the top along with "Mary Poppins" and "My Fair Lady." Both new and traditional films were at the top of the charts. Nikos Kazantzakis' book, *Zorba, the Greek* was also made into a very popular film in that year as one of the first truly popular foreign films on the American screen. Out of these, it was "My Fair Lady" that won the Oscar.

On stage, "Hello, Dolly" opened in New York, as did "Fiddler on the Roof." Both of these plays also contributed their theme songs to the most popular of the year. If you remember all this important pop-culture trivia you will remember that "You've come a long way, baby!"

New Mexico in 1964 had a Democratic Governor by the name of Jack M. Campbell. Some of you might remember that he beat Edward L. Mecham and served two terms as governor. Mecham had been governor three times before but Campbell was the first governor in many years to serve two back-to-back terms. Governors only served for two years at that time. Just after Campbell, gubernatorial terms were extended to four years. McKinley and San Juan Counties sent their first Navajo representatives to the state legislature that year also. Among our Congressional delegation in Washington, representing our district was Congressman Joseph M. Montoya of Bernalillo. He served as our representative from 1957 until 1964, when he resigned to fill the Senate vacancy left by the death of Dennis Chavez. He continued to serve as senator until 1977.

During this time of unrest across the country, there was activity here in New Mexico as well. The protests here did not relate to "Free Speech" or the Vietnam War. The protests here had to do with *La Alianza Federal de Mercedes* which had been organized the year before by Reies Lopez Tijerina. The issue here was similar to the general civil rights battle taking place across the country. The main issue here had to do with land use rather than the right to vote or the color of our skin. At this same time, there also began a huge migration of "Hippies" into northern New Mexico where these uninvited guests began to establish their own communes. These young people were a very diverse group from many places. They were not familiar with the peoples of northern New Mexico or our traditions. They were not accepted or welcome in the communities in or around which they had decided to "commune with nature," while living in their tents and colorful busses. Cuba had its share of Hippie experiences, as did places like Taos and Placitas and other communities off the beaten path.

Fifty years ago, Cuba, New Mexico, was humming with activity. Richard's Barber Shop advertised in the High School Yearbook, "We cut hair to please YOU, not ourselves;" a recognition of changing styles and youthful independence. According to another ad, one could also "Dine in the relaxing atmosphere of the Wagon Wheel Cafe." There was a full-service drug store owned by Mr. and Mrs. Standridge, a First State Bank, Cosmo's Oil Company, Freeloves' all-purpose general store, the Midway Bar and Lounge and numerous other businesses.

According to the Immaculate Conception School archive, in May of 1964, seventy-six children went through the Confirmation ceremony. It is also stated that there were two hundred thirty students enrolled at this school that year.

Those of you who made your First Holy Communion or were Confirmed in 1964 were the last of Cuba's population to do so in our 1915 church. A new era was beginning in Cuba. In May, 1964, while the Bishop was in town presiding over Confirmation, he "addressed the congregation on the need of erecting a new church." Documents that followed say that the last mass at the old church was celebrated on February 14, 1965 and shortly after that, the beloved, fifty-year-old church was razed. Certainly, this was the beginning of a new era in Cuba's Catholic community. Earlier, it was said that 1964 was "a year to remember." Perhaps for some parishioners, it was a year they never forgot.

At Cuba High School there was a Biology Club, a Science Club, a yearbook and a student newspaper. There was also a Drill Team with no less than forty members in white blouses and dark jumpers. Keep in mind that this was 1964.

In addition to the many clubs there were football, basketball and wrestling teams plus two or three cheerleading squads. A Letterman's Club is pictured in the yearbook with at least sixteen proud male members. Did the female athletes not get letters? How were they recognized? In looking through the yearbook, it appears as if there were no girls' teams in basketball or volleyball. Perhaps that is why there were so many cheerleaders and so many girls on the Drill Team. Affirmative action laws regarding sports for girls were still more than twenty years away.

The thirty-three seniors shown in the yearbook were probably rocking and rolling to Elvis Presley or perhaps two-stepping to the latest country music at the beginning of the year. However, Beatlemania had begun and was probably the rage by prom time. Along with the Beatles' music, everyone would have been trying to learn how to dance the "Watusi," the "Funky Chicken," or other versions of the "Twist." By 1964, there were enough television sets in Cuba that no one would miss American Bandstand. Everyone would have been up on all the latest dance styles.

Fifty years later there are no more than five of the thirty-three graduates of 1964 still living in Cuba. Two of the female graduates, Theresa Duran and Elaine Valdez Velarde have their own businesses. Not one of the male members of this promising class still lives in Cuba. Joseph Gurulé, while he was still alive, was the only one who stayed here through his adulthood, serving his community.

In January 1964, Bob Dylan sang *The Times They Are a-Changin'* and certainly they did. Will the Class of '64 have a fiftieth class reunion? This would be their golden anniversary, the color of their yearbook. Like the rest of us, what must they think of all the changes that have taken place in fifty years? What has happened to their dreams?

The rest of us also experienced at least some of those events and some of us experienced even more. Much has changed over these fifty years. Some changes have been good and others have not met our expectations. There have been many surprises in our lives and things we did not expect or count on.

Along with "Beatlemania," there is a lot for us to reflect on and think about after so many years. Incidentally, to my knowledge, the Cuba High School Class of 1964 did not have a class reunion to celebrate the fiftieth anniversary of their graduation.

PART II

Pláticas de Tristezas y Amor
(Conversations
about Sadness
and Love)

These Conversations consists of three basic elements: eulogies, elegies, and poems. There are actual eulogies I wrote and presented at the time deaths occurred. A eulogy is defined as a speech or writing in praise of a person, event or thing; especially a formal speech praising a person who has recently died. It could also be high praise or commendation or a tribute.

Elegies are the second component of this section. These are pieces out of my personal journals and writings of commemoration and lament, again, following the deaths of many former students, friends and relatives. Originally, elegies were written in poetic form. Not all of my commemorations are in the form of poems, although some are. Some are simply statements of deep lament following the deaths of people I have loved and who touched my life in a special way.

The elegies written in poetic form make up the third section. Even though I am not formally a writer of poetry, "Free form poetry" has become a very well accepted form of literature used widely today. Some of these poems are written in Spanish. Some adapt to translation and some may not. Spanish is my first language and in times of deep grief or emotional stress I revert to expressing my thoughts in that language.

Over the time that I taught at Cuba Independent Schools, I soon became sadly aware of the number of deaths that were occurring among former students and young people in general. In a state of deep sorrow over the loss of these young people, I began to keep a list of the deaths of what were to me the loss of precious lives who were leaving a huge void in my life. These were losses that affected not only the young people's families. It affected many of us who had nurtured these young people at school or as family. Ultimately, their deaths were a deprivation of their potential to the community at large.

In my entire career as a teacher, the most difficult undertaking I endured following the death of one of our young people was to give my condolences to the parents and families of students I had loved and witnessed their potential toward success. It is out of this close, almost daily contact with these people that some of these writings arose and can now be shared. Over the years, there were so many of these deaths that I eventually stopped writing names on what I referred to as "a List of the Dead." I simply continued to write about them and mourn their passing.

Eulogy for Alex Montoya and Ernie Cordova.

My dear cousins Ernest, Fabiola and Frank; my dear, dear friends Rae, Arthur and Andrea: in the words of Emily Dickenson, I quote:

> Its all I have to bring to-day,
> This, and my heart beside,
> This and my heart, and all the fields,
> And all of the meadows wide
> Be sure you count, should I forget, ...
> Some one the sum could tell, ...
> This, and my heart, and all the bees
> Which in the clover dwell.

Friends,

Alex and Ernie lived in a world filled with love, friendship and caring. It is because of this love, our friendships and caring that we are all here today. It is what gives meaning to this gathering and what once again binds our saddened community together.

Ernie's and Alex's spirits have been set free. They have lived. And now each of us will recall their beautiful lives as we each shared in those lives. Yet, in common, we will all recall the joy in those wonderful smiles. We will recall how easily and how genuinely each of them laughed. We will, for a long, long time remember the sparkle in their eyes, sometimes a little mischievous. Most of all we will recall, what my husband Don described as the exuberance with which they each approached life.

In varying degrees, we have known these young men. We have also loved them, and because they loved us, we each have an obligation to their memory, to continue to love each other. As their family, their classmates, friends, teachers and as their community, we have painfully met the ultimate challenge, death. We have overcome. And now, we collectively, who loved Alex and Ernie must, in their honor, celebrate LIFE.

I would like to close with a poem by the Spanish poet, Juan Ramon Jimenez. The poem is titled, *El Viaje Definitivo*.

El Viaje Definitivo

. . . Y yo me iré. Y se quedarán los pájaros cantando;
y se quedará mi huerto, con su verde árbol,
y con su pozo blanco.

Todas las tardes, el cielo será azul y plácido;
y tocarán, como esta tarde están tocando,
las campanas del campanario.

Se murirán aquellos que me amaron;
y el pueblo se hará nuevo cada año;
y en el rincón aquel de mi huerto florido y encalado,
mi espíritu errará; nostálgico . . .

Y yo me iré; y estaré solo, sin hogar, sin árbol
verde, sin pozo blanco,
sin cielo azul y plácido . . .
y se quedarán los pájaros cantando.

Alex and Ernie were on their way back from Las Cruces, where they had gone to arrange for student housing and register for their third year of classes at New Mexico State University. Less than twenty minutes from home, they were caught in a horrific downpour on what was then the two-lane Highway 44. Their vehicle went out of control, veering straight into one of the many arroyos in the area. They had lived in friendship and died together as friends. Both of these bright, promising young men had been my students and I was deeply honored when asked to give their eulogy.

(Written by Esther Cordova May, delivered at the funeral service in Cuba New Mexico on July 28, 1994. Published with the consent of the families: Ernest and Fabiola Cordova and Arthur and Rae Montoya.)

Eulogy for Emma Adelina DeLaO

Another eulogy included here that I was honored to deliver was for one of my mother's younger sisters, a person I literally grew up with. As the last member of my mother's siblings, her death has left a huge void in my life and part of the deep sadness referred to in the title of this chapter.

Muy buenos días les de Dios. Gracias que nos an acompañado durant esta ocasión. Triste naturalmente pero necesaria. La familia agradese su presencia y su amistad.

My name is Esther Cordova May. I am Emma's oldest niece. Sadly, my Aunt Emma's death not only marks the end of a generation of our family; it is also the end of an era. An era which illustrated what is meant to be loved and cared for unconditionally.

With Emma's death, my *primos hermanos,* my first cousins, and I have lost the last member of a family that loved us from the day we were born and in return, we loved them just like our Grandma Genara and our Grandpa Eduardo had taught us all to love and care for each other.

Emma Adelina De La O was born on Easter Sunday, April 5, 1931. She was the seventh of eight children in the Eduardo De La O family. There were six females and two males. Amadeo was nearly six years old when he died of diphtheria. My mother was the oldest member of that generation, followed by Edwina, Francisco (Frank), and Amadeo. After Amadeo's death, Josephine was born prematurely, requiring a great deal of care so that she would survive to adulthood. In 1927, Lydia was born. She was barely four when Emma came along in 1931. The youngest member of this family, Rosie, followed shortly after in 1933, giving Emma a very short babyhood.

I am only three years younger than Rose and Emma was only five when I was born in 1936. The early part of my childhood was spent among all these women and my fondest memories of love, care and happiness are with them and my grandparents.

Our Aunt Emma originally had twenty-four nieces and nephews. Ten of these belonged to our Uncle Frank, who left home in search of work when he was about sixteen years old. He lived in California when he was drafted at the age of eighteen at the beginning of World War II. His children were all born in California after the war, as were my aunt Rose's four children. My Aunt Edwina Montoya's four boys and I grew up together with Rose, Lydia and Emma. Aunt Josephine was busy finishing high school, Uncle Patricio and my Dad were in the service and Grandpa was away a lot working in sheep camps in Wyoming, Colorado and Utah. With no males to help Grandma with the feeding of animals, planting and harvesting Emma became our Grandmother's dependable right-hand helper. She would chop wood and feed the horses and cows. She was not afraid of any job that Grandma would ask her to do. For instance, she could chop the head off a chicken or kill and skin a rabbit needed for dinner. She was smart, strong and dedicated to her mother.

In those days, there used to be a six o'clock mass every morning which Grandma attended and Emma would accompany her, no matter how deep the snow was or how cold it was. I don't recall that Grandma ever had to wake Emma up: they were both early risers. They would attend Mass fasting, as was required back then, have communion and then walk the two miles back home for breakfast and then Emma would get ready for school.

Emma was a good student and loved school. She was particularly good in science and was mechanically inclined. She loved tools and knew how to use them creatively. Emma was the first among us to learn how to ride a bike. Cousin Clyde Montoya got a bike, probably through our *Tío* Celestino but this was not the kind of bike we saw in the Sear's catalogue. This was an English bike with really narrow wheels and a hand brake. Hand brakes on bikes were something none of the rest of us knew anything about. Emma apparently did, given that she got on it and knew what to do. That was the way she was as we were growing up.

Lydia had graduated from high school in 1946 and immediately left for Albuquerque to look for a job. By the fall of 1948, it became obvious that our local Convent School would not be able to maintain its high school program. Emma and Rose went to live with Lydia while they attended and graduated from St. Mary's High School. Looking at the few pictures of Emma among her friends during her St. Mary's days, I believe these may have been the happiest and most carefree days of her life. She was free to be a student and excelled during those two years.

Following her graduation and much to everyone's surprise, Emma decided to become a Franciscan nun in 1949. This was also my first year away at boarding school. I remember crying at night for Emma because she was then so far away and I knew even then that life would never be the same for either of us again.

Emma must have spent about fifteen years in the Convent and, to my knowledge, only had one home visit during that time, which would have been around 1964. By then, Grandpa and Grandma were in California, living with Uncle Frank's family. I was also living in California and this was the first time I had seen Emma since the fall of 1949.

At some point in her Convent days, Emma was allowed to attend the prestigious Creighton University in Omaha where she graduated with honors in chemistry. She then became a professional medical lab technician, working in hospitals.

In the middle or late 1960s, Emma left the Convent, returned to Albuquerque and began a whole new phase of her life. Immediately and with the patient help of Uncle Pat, she learned to drive and bought a car. She worked two full-time jobs and soon had enough money to purchase a house not far from her sister Edwina and her family and arranged for Grandpa and Grandma to live with her. With our grandparents back in New Mexico, that house became the headquarters for all who travelled back and forth, whether from Cuba, Cañon or California. The door was always open and we were free to stay as long as we needed or wanted to stay.

During that time, Emma did many unexpected things. She learned to ski when she was well over thirty years old. While cousin Clyde and family lived in Montana, she drove there to visit them. She also went to

California several times and enjoyed the many cars she owned during this period. She also took up photography and woodworking with great ambition.

In 1971, after Grandma died, my mother and Aunt Josephine arranged for Grandpa to return to Cuba. Emma remained in Albuquerque until she retired and eventually moved to the beautiful Jemez Valley. This is where so many of you here today got to know her.

She remained steadfast in her attitudes and life style throughout her later years, including her rigorous, self-imposed fitness program and her visiting the sick and the elderly. (She did not think of herself as sick or elderly.) This was not always easy for some of us to deal with, either family members or the other well-meaning people in her life. However, all of us, her nieces and nephews and dear cousins, tried to look beyond the difficulties of getting along with her and loved her for who she was. She was, after all, our aunt and she was family. Our mothers and our grandparents would have wanted us to do that. For any others whom she may have offended, we hope you can do the same and on her behalf, we are sorry.

Now, after this long, active and sometimes unsettled life, she is at peace. While we will miss her, we can know that she did what she could do for those around her, generally with good intentions, and that the time has come for her to rest. I can just hear Grandma asking, *¿Porque te tardaste tanto, hija? Te estábamos esperando.* And so was the life of Emma Adelina DeLaO. Our sincere thanks to Gloria and Michael Martinez for seeing her through her last days. They were gracious and helpful beyond measure. *¡Gracias!*

(Delivered at the funeral mass at Santo Toribio Church, Ponderosa, New Mexico, December 3, 2016.)

Emma DeLaO, happy student at St. Mary's High School.

Elegy in Memory of Celso Montoya

Celso and I retired from Cuba Independent Schools together in May, 1996, where I had gotten to know him and work with him. Over the years as I worked along side Celso, I found him to have a positive outlook on life in general, even when faced with undaunting challenges. Furthermore, he had a marvelous sense of humor. Above all, he enjoyed the students and took every opportunity to be helpful and kind to all students and coworkers. Celso's legacy revolved around his family, his active role as the leader of the *Guadalupanos* and his music. Among his many accolades, in 1997 he was awarded the New Mexico Traditional Hispanic Folk Music Award. Locally, the gymnasium at Cuba High School was named and dedicated in his honor.

For those of us who had the privilege of knowing Celso, it is not difficult to understand how the following elegy became a lament for a man whose death left a deep void in a community that loved him.

Many years ago, a teacher at Cuba Middle School was doing a lesson on heroes and on people the students admired. After some discussion about kinds of qualities these heroes possessed, the students were given time to write a short assignment about the people they admired.

Later, after the students completed the assignment, the teacher was glancing over the papers and discovered that one of the students had put down Celso Montoya as the person he most admired. The teacher was impressed by the child's admiration of Celso and called him up to her desk and asked him to elaborate on what he had written.

The student then confidently explained to the teacher that the reasons he admired him were because Celso did a lot of good things for people all the time and that "Celso was not only very nice, he was sort of like a saint."

It has been a long time since this incident occurred. However, I never forgot how clear this young person's vision of Celso had been. Over the years, as I got to know Celso better, I too understood more completely what this child had seen in the friend we all loved and admired so much. Indeed, we all loved him because "he was not only very nice, he was sort of like a saint."

(This elegy is taken from my personal journal, written on March 12, 1998, in memory of Celso R. Montoya following his death on March 5, 1998. Published with the consent of Nestorita Montoya, Celso's wife.)

Celso R. Montoya. The man seen from the eyes of a child, "sort of like a saint."
Cuba High School Yearbook, 1998.

Elegy for "Little Marshall"

In the fall of 1991, a boy came to Cuba Middle School. A boy with a great big smile and deep, dark eyes. A boy whose slender body hadn't quite grown as much, or as fast, as his face and head. A boy whose smile remained constant, as were his cousins and ardent companions, the twins Peter and Paul Cebada.

It was rare that Marshall was ever seen alone in sixth grade, or later in seventh and eighth grades. Marshall was well liked by his classmates and by his many friends. The adults at school, those of us who had known Marshall since early childhood, loved him. We also watched over him and probably doted upon him. He knew we were doting and he would smile and go about his business with Peter, Paul or Jared Maestas at his side.

Marshall was one of those young people who was liked by everyone because he was such a pleasant person to have around. The result was, we enjoyed him, and we watched him grow up.

I believe that early on Saturday morning, November 4, 1995, his mother (who had preceded him in death many years before) wanted him with her. We had cherished her "Little Marshall" for a while. We had enjoyed him immensely and now he can spend eternity with her. After all, he was hers first.

Those of us who knew and loved "Little Marshall" still have the memory of his broad smile, his sparkling black eyes and that little look he had that said, "Its okay for you to love me; I understand."

The loss of Marshall to his family and his friends is painful but it is also an honor to know that during his short life, Marshall always gave each of us who loved him a warm smile and a feeling of wellbeing. I felt good when I encountered Marshall, not because of anything I did but because of who he was: a "neat kid."

Post Script: "Little Marshall's" dear friend Jared Maestas and his wife Anita have four children. They have two daughters and two sons. The older of the two boys is named after Jared's childhood friend, Marshall Lucero, Jr. and is called "Little Marshall." Marshall was a mere passenger in a vehicle involved in an accident. He was only sixteen years old at the time of his death.

(From my personal journal dated, Saturday, November 4, 1995. Published with the permission of John Lucero, Marshall's oldest brother and Jared and Anita Maestas, parents of the new "Little Marshall.")

"Little Marshal," the charmer." Cuba High School Yearbook, 1996.

Elegy for Natalia

I was one of Natalia's teachers at Cuba Middle School and I loved this child. I had also been her older siblings' teacher and loved each one of the four I had taught before her. Since Natalia was a twin, in those days we separated twins and so I never got to teach her twin sister. Lupe would have been in the other section of seventh and eighth grade. A blessing for those of us who knew and loved Natalia as a youngster and as a young adult: bright, full of life, beaming with energy and not too infrequently, oh! so full of mischief. These are our fond memories of Natalia, who will remain forever young.

The following three verses are from a Bob Dylan song titled "Forever Young." Subsequent to Natalia's agonizing death, caused by extensive burn injuries, I thought Bob Dylan's words were an appropriate way to recall Natalia. I quote:

> May God bless and keep you always,
> May your wishes all come true,
> May you always do for others
> And let others do for you.
>
> May you build a ladder to the stars,
> And climb on every rung,
> May you stay
> Forever young.
>
> May your heart always be joyful,
> May your song always be sung,
> May you stay
> Forever young,
> Forever young.

For those of us whose lives you brightened for such a brief life-time with your youthful smile, your thoughtfulness and charm, we will remember you. In turn, we will recount lovingly to your darling daughters how you have remained forever young.

In my journal, I also found a Post-It note that reads: Natalia, thank you for the rain on the day you were laid to rest in your ancestral home of La Jara. The note has to do with the fact that 2004 had been a particularly dry year and on the day of Natalia's funeral, it actually rained.

(From my personal journal, dated June 23, 2004. Published with the consent of Elisea Maestas, Natalia's mother.)

You will remain forever young in the minds of all who knew you.

Elegy for a Middle Child

She was the middle child. She was beloved by her three older siblings and adored by her three younger sisters. It is said that she was born prematurely. As was the custom in those long-ago days, she spent the first few weeks of her life in a bag filled with warm wheat bran at her mother's breast. Carefully watched and indulged due to her delicate start,
She was beloved and adored.

She grew up strong, robust, happy, healthy and accustomed to the special attention she had been privileged to as an infant.
She was beloved and adored.

She was named Josefina, after her mother's younger sister. Josefina had been a very young, healthy mother of three children when her life was cut short in the dark and horrible winter of 1918. Obviously, even by July, 1924, she had not been forgotten by a loving sister when the next Josefina was born.

Beloved and adored.

The beautiful Josefina smiled generously. She laughed easily.
She spoke loudly and always ate heartily.
In that safe, comfortable circle of sisters, nieces, cousins and her precious daughter,
she was our brightest star.
Beloved and adored.

In life, she could not keep a secret. She loved music, would sing out loud,
dance when she felt the urge. She simply had a contagious zest for life.
She left as she had lived: cared for and indulged, knowing she had always been special.
She was the middle child.
Beloved and adored.

In Loving memory of
Josefina DeLaO Lucero.
She smiled generously,
She laughed easily,
She spoke loudly,
She lived fully,
She died in the fullness of life:
Special!

(From my personal journal, 28 November, 2001. Published with the consent of her daughter, Prexie Lucero.)

Josefina (middle), with youngest sister Rose and their mother Genara DeLaO, circa 1971.
She smiled so generously!

Poems

In Memory of Chris, a Good Boy

    I brought you white flowers
at our last encounter, out of my own needs and pain.
    White flowers I had cut from my own precious greenhouse
plants.
    out of my own needs and pain.

    I brought you white flowers
in a round, crystal clear vase
like a baptismal gift,
because in my mind, you were
        gentle,
        kind,
        thoughtful and
        loving;
despite the pain you had endured during the few years
you lived your quiet life.

    I brought you white flowers
in a round, crystal clear vase
because you were more precious
than my greenhouse plants.

    I brought you white flowers
you would never see,
out of my own need
out of my own pain
and out of love for the

quiet
gentle
kind and
generous boy
you will always be
in my thoughts
and in my mind.

I brought you my precious white flowers
in a round, crystal clear vase
because I cared
and didn't do enough for the
gentle
quiet
kind boy
that lives in my thoughts
and in my mind.

I still have white flowers but
the quiet, gentle boy is no more.

Postscript: Chris had been my student. He had such an inwardly beautiful, gentle soul that I absolutely loved. I knew he had suffered many indignities and lots of pain. Sadly, he was not my child and I could not bring him home with me and care for him. Chris is one of those truly gentle people for whom I regret not having intervened more openly in his behalf.

Chris died very tragically on March 25, 1997.

(From my 1998 Personal Journal.)

Sadness
(For my cousin, Dino Gutierrez)

> A child of sorrow
> died in May.
>
> A victim of the social ills
> of the day.
>
> A child grown into a boy
> lived tragically, violently and sad.
>
> A victim of the social ills
> of the day.
>
> A child born in
> the brilliant green of a
> California spring, born in despair
> enveloped only by the thin web
> of his mother's love.
>
> A victim of the social ills
> of the day.
>
> A boy grown into a man
> lived dangerously, violently and sad,
> shielded only by the thin web
> of his mother's love.

A child of sorrow
a boy of sadness
a man of violence
died in May.

A victim of the social ills
of the day.

A man of sadness died in May,
shielded only by the thin web
of his mother's love
on Mothers' Day!

A victim of the social ills
of the day.

Dino was murdered in his mother's house on Mothers' Day, May 13, 2001.

(From my personal journal, dated May 14, 2001. Published with the permission of the only surviving member of Dino's immediate family, his sister Judy Meadows.)

Elegía Para Matthew Cordova

No hay consuelo ninguno
Para el padre
Al ver el cuerpo de su hijo:
Sin respiro
Sin habla
Sin sonrisa.

No hay consuelo ninguno
Para el joven
Al ver el cuerpo de su hermano
Caído
Sin habla
Sin sonrisa

No habra consuelo ninguno
Para el pueblo
Que pierde a un consentido
Regoldando de vida, fuerte, gracioso
Y lleno de sonrisa.
No habra consuelo ninguno

Note: Matthew had been my student in eighth grade. A young man with a smile that could fill a room. I loved Matthew and his easy, good-natured manner. Gentle but so easily led. The circumstances under which Matthew was shot to death were never made clear to me. What was clear was that Matthew, gentle and full of life, was dead. Dead unnecessarily one month before his eighteenth birthday

Later, in 2010, I went back to visit this elegy and added:
En paz, en las manos de Dios.

(From my personal journal, Thursday, June 6, 1996, evening. Published with the consent of Abram A. Cordova, Jr., Matthew's father, who prefers that this piece not be translated.)

On the Road to Coyote

For My Father, Ruben Cordova:
November 13, 1997

Snow-flocked trees
Along the way,
Under a gray, cloudy sky
Entrance into a dream

Distant mountains under
A thin blanket of snow,
Pedernal wearing a headdress
of cloud. Prominence is hers.

Pedernal, Mesa del Frances
Distant mountains under
A thin blannket of snow
Land that my father loved.

Land and mountains his fathers claimed
Land and mountains that still pull
At my soul like something long remembered,
Like the moon draws the tides.

Snow-flocked trees
Along the way,
Under a gray, cloudy sky.
Entrance into a dream,
A distant dream pulling at my soul.

Pedernal Peak, between Coyote and Abiquiu, New Mexico.

A Beautiful Dream

(A Dream in Progress as I Woke Up:
7 a.m., Saturday, February 15, 1993)

In my vivid dream, you, Vincent my love,
You are a normal man.

In my vivid dream, you, Vincent young man,
You have faculties like everyone else.

In my dreams, Vincent,
My highest hopes become reality.

Though rare, these special vivid dreams
have been of you, of you, the normal man.
I treasure them and continue to believe
that through some technological miracle
you will some day have faculties
like everyone else.

I will continue to dream.
I will continue to hope.

I will continue to believe that
my most wonderful dreams of you
can become reality.

I will continue to dream.
to dream vivid dreams of you,
of you, a normal man.

Vincent May, seven years old, looking at a goldfish at a day school for disabled children.

"I love snow!" Vincent May on vacation at Kings Canyon National Park, California, 1975.

PART III

Pláticas Formal Presentadadas a Audiencias
(Formal Presentations to an Audience)

Una Plática de Parentela
(A Conversation About Ancestry)

(Adapted from a Sandoval County Historical Society presentation, June, 2012)

I knew when I began this *Plática* that it had the potential of being con-troversial, or even disputed because I am introducing the possibility of Crypto-Judaism as a part of our heritage. Yet, while doing the research, I found the material increasingly more interesting and felt more compelled to express my thoughts on the subject of *parentela*.

I was born and raised in Cuba, New Mexico, as were both of my parents, my maternal grandparents and my paternal grandmother. As expected of children of my era, I grew up knowing who my relatives were "unto the seventh generation." For instance, I knew that all the Córdovas from Cuba were related to me and descended from one family, a situation that continued to exist until very recently. The history of how it came to be this way is, in effect, mine and my many cousins' "legacy." I happened to be fortunate in that my mother, her sisters and female cousins were *las reinas de la plática* (queens of conversation) and I was privileged to hear the same stories over and over again about who we were on that side of the family. My father, Ruben Cordova, on the other hand, came from such a dysfunctional family following the death of his mother that he had learned very early in life who all his relatives were in Cuba, Gallina and points beyond, in order to survive. He too had learned and listened to the stories of ancestry many times over and had a good grasp of his family history. These stories, too, I listened to repeatedly every time a member of the Cordova family stopped at our house on their way to, or coming from Gallina, Coyote or Capulín. Unlike my father, I had learned about my Cordova ancestry under much more pleasant circumstances than his. We simply went to visit our relatives in Gallina and Los Pinos and I was left with very fond memories of those families we did continue to have contact with as I was growing up.

In Fray Angelico Chavez's *Origins of New Mexico Families*, his short entry of the Córdoba family goes back to Señor Antonio de Córdoba, a notary, a native of Mexico City. Webster's *New World Dictionary* says "notary" is short for Notary Public. A Notary Public, as defined both in English and Spanish sources is "an official authorized to certify or attest documents; take depositions and affidavits." The Spanish definition goes as far as to say, "as confirmed by the laws."

Given these definitions of Señor Córdoba's occupation, we can assume he must have been highly literate, had some knowledge of the law and was likely licensed to do his work.

Although a native of Mexico City, apparently, he did not remain there. The question then arises as to why he was at Guadalupe del Paso (now, El Paso, Texas) in 1695. According to Fray Angelico Chavez, Señor Antonio de Córdoba while in Guadalupe del Paso was still acting as a notary and had also married Eugenia de Herrera, who had been born in New Mexico before the Pueblo Revolt of 1680.

This suggests that Señor Antonio de Córdoba was migrating northward and perhaps even attempting to get to New Mexico.

Records also show that he and his wife, Eugenia de Herrera had two children, a son, Lazaro Antonio and a daughter, Ana Maria.

Adventure does not seem to be the motive for Señor Antonio's migration northward. As a point of reference, these events would have been taking place two years or more following the De Vargas expedition of 1693 and the reconquest of New Mexico, making it the northern-most province of New Spain.

Historically, we know that there was a large colony of New Mexicans in Guadalupe del Paso who survived the Pueblo Revolt. These former New Mexicans were awaiting an opportunity to return and reclaim their properties in New Mexico from before the revolt. Eugenia de Herrera was among those native New Mexicans who had property to claim. According to Chavez, "Eugenia and her brother Miguel owned land jointly in Santa Cruz de la Cañada." Again, according to records provided by Chavez, between 1712 and 1762, Lazaro, son of Don Antonio, is listed in land documents in the Santa Cruz or Rio Arriba areas of New Mexico. By this time, Lazaro would have been an adult and, since his mother had been born in New Mexico, probably held title to lands belonging to his mother's family. By this time, some sources say Don Antonio was listed as deceased.

My theory on why Señor Antonio de Córdoba was seemingly eluding detection in Mexico City is because I believe he was of Jewish ancestry. Do recall that records show he was a native of Mexico City, which means he had been born there, he had a profession that required an education and a business that was probably very lucrative. Unfortunately, we do not know how old he was when he reached Guadalupe del Paso. What we do know is that he was old enough to marry, have children and continue to practice his profession. Personally, I don't think he was particularly out to make money off of new clients.

Given the three hundred plus years between the beginning of this *Plática* and today, some could say my theory is based on mere speculation related to Señor Antonio de Córdoba's Crypto-Judaism. Yet, there are enough historical shreds of evidence of the dangers and realities of that time that he would have been subjected to as a Jew. These bits of information give credence to my efforts to piece the events and people involved into a family narrative.

What leads me to pursue these shreds of evidence is examples such as the following information. According to Michael C. Meyers and William L. Sherman in their book, *The Course of Mexican History*, they say that by 1571, religion became more important in New Spain. It was at this time that the Holy Office of the Inquisition arrived in New Spain. It would have been an event like the brutal implementation of these laws that would cause young, educated Jews like Antonio de Córdoba to be on the march as far away from Mexico City as possible. Authors Meyers and Sherman emphasize two important points as related to Jews in New Spain. One was that emigrants to the new world were screened before leaving Spain to make sure there were no Jews or *Conversos* (converts referred to as "new Catholics") emigrating to New Spain. The second thing these authors emphasize is that "the Inquisition that was dispatched to Mexico City was determined to root out Crypto-Jews in New Spain."

It is important to remember that the Inquisition in Spain was established in 1480 and had been ruthlessly practiced for 91 years before enforcement began in New Spain in 1571. Amazingly, these laws were not abolished until 1821 when Mexico gained independence from Spain.

Consistent with data from Angelico Chavez, Eugenia de Herrera Córdoba and her children seem to have arrived safely in Santa Cruz de la Cañada in New Mexico. Sources vary on whether Señor Antonio de Córdoba actually got to New Mexico himself. We do not know if the family stayed for a time in the Santa Cruz area and whether, as some sources state, had the nearby settlement of Cordova named after them. One point seems clear. This family, for what ever reasons, was staying in the area designated as Rio Arriba. I would like to say that these people seemingly continued to attempt to move even farther northward.

The 1880 census of the population of Gallina and Capulín, New Mexico, (the area just north of Cuba) records that my great-grandfather, Pascual Córdoba and his brother Antonio lived in that area but were born in Taos. These two brothers were married to two sisters from the sizeable Jaquez family and apparently the two families travelled together. Antonio married Ignacita Jaquez and Pascual married Maria Doloritas Jaquez. Interestingly, this same 1880 census records that the two brothers' older children had been born in Culebra, a Hispanic settlement in the San Luis Valley of what became Colorado. According to this census, the younger children in these families were all born in Coyote, New Mexico, a tiny settlement located between Abiquiu and Gallina, in the mid to late 1870s.

It is very likely that these two brothers had been part of numerous attempts made by many northern Hispanic families to settle permanently in the San Luis Valley. These efforts failed because Native tribes who already occupied that land repeatedly pushed the Hispanics back into the safety of the Abiquiu area. Eventually, the Anglo invasion from the east settled the issue. Given the resources of fertile land and unlimited water in the San Luis Valley and the rich coal deposits in the Trinidad area were very desirable to the expanding United States. Congress was quick to declare Colorado a state in 1876 with its southern boundary set at latitude 37 degrees. This boundary includes both the San Luis Valley and the coal deposits within the new state. Given the information gleaned from the 1880 census, it appears the mid-1870s was about the time the Córdoba brothers and their families returned to the Rio Arriba area to find a new place to live and continue their subsistence ranching lifestyle.

Pascual and Antonio Córdoba remained in the Gallina and Capulín area where, in 1887, they helped establish the first Presbyterian church in that area. They accomplished this with the blessing and authority of the Reverend Dr. J. M. Shields, the missionary doctor who established many of the Presbyterian churches in northern New Mexico, including the Jemez Springs Presbyterian Church. The entire Córdoba clan and their in-laws are listed in the official register as original members of the Capulín Spanish Presbyterian Church. Note that the family was still using the spelling of Córdoba with a "b" but had dropped the "de," which indicated that they might have been from the ancient city of Córdoba in Spain.

This dramatic mass enrollment of the entire family into the Presbyterian Church is in my opinion further evidence that this Córdoba family was of Jewish ancestry. They did not establish this church as converts from Catholicism. According to the initial church record, they did so with a letter of transfer from the Presbyterian Church in Jemez Springs, which means they were already practicing Presbyterians when they came to Capulín and Gallina.

Stanley M. Hordes, in his book, *To the Ends of the Earth*, claims that following the signing of the Treaty of Guadalupe Hidalgo in 1848, and the American takeover of New Mexico guaranteed Mexican citizens "free exercise of their religion without restriction." "Without restriction" now meant access to the Bible, which had been strictly forbidden under Spanish law and the Catholic Church. Hordes further states, "Hispanos who had held on to their Jewish traditions were drawn to Presbyterianism because it afforded them access to sacred texts." As well, there was the very important factor that, as in Judaism, Presbyterianism emphasizes a direct relationship with God, thus eliminating the need for intercession by either priests or Saints as well as a priest's explanation of biblical text.

According to the official record of the Capulín Spanish Presbyterian Church, it was organized with fourteen members on March 16, 1887. José

Antonio Córdoba was chosen Ruling Elder, by Rumaldo Montoya, who was Ruling Elder in the Jemez Springs Church. "On the 6th day of April, the Church of Capulín was received by the Presbytery of Santa Fé, then in Session."

Of the fourteen original members of the Capulín Spanish Presbyterian Church, nine of these original members were Córdobas, along with nineteen-year-old Epimenia Córdoba Duran, daughter of Pascual, who was already married to Leonardo Duran and both of them are part of the original membership. Marino and Josefa, Pascual and Dolorita's other two children, became members of the church in 1887 and 1888. Marino was only eight years old at the time. Antonio and Ingacita Córdoba had fifteen children according to my sources and continued to add to the church membership as the children became of age. Antonio remained an Elder of the Capulín Church until July 18, 1926, when he died at the age of 79.

In 1889, my great-grandfather, Pascual Córdoba and part of his family came over the mountain from the Gallina-Capulín area into the upper Rio Puerco valley. There, he homesteaded one hundred sixty acres of land where he and his family lived. This area, just north of Cuba, is generally referred to as Los Pinos. Some of Pascual's family still live on the original homestead.

Pascual and Doloritas' family consisted of four sons who would perpetuate the Córdoba name. They also had two daughters. If our name is Córdoba and we are from Cuba, we all grew up knowing Los Pinos was where our ancestral roots were.

Pascual's oldest son was Lugardo. Incidentally, Lugardo was one of the Córdoba children born in Culebra in 1873, while the Córdoba brothers were trying to settle in the San Luis Valley. Lugardo and his wife, Trinidad Vigil Córdoba only had one son and one daughter, Danué and Rebeca. Francisco had three daughters and two sons. He and his first wife, Leonor Lucero Córdoba had Ruben, Elzira and Teresita. Following Leonor's untimely death in 1918, Francisco and his second wife, Antonia Ortega Córdoba, had Eloyda and Elí. Marino had only one son, Amadeo and a daughter, Dolores.

Julian ad his wife, Julia Cebada Córdoba, formed the largest part of the Pascual branch of the family. This family consisted of six male children and three females. Several of these Julian offspring have had large families so the name Córdoba has been widely perpetuated in Cuba.

The two daughters in the Pascual branch of the family were Josefa and Epimenia Córdoba Duran. Epimenia, like Lugardo, was born in the San Luis Valley in 1868. Recall that in 1887, when the Capulín Church was established, she was already married to Leonardo Duran, both having been listed among the fourteen original members of that church. Unfortunately, there are no other references with information about them. In the following generation, a daughter named Adela Duran married Esequiel Padilla in La Ventana, New Mexico (fifteen miles south of Cuba), where the family settled. Currently, there are still members of Adela and Esequiel's family who ranch in La Ventana. According to Esequiel Padilla, Jr. Epimenia died in 1933, at which time her husband, Leonardo, came to live with Adela's family in La Ventana until his death in 1945.

The other daughter, Josefa, married Juan Basilio Archuleta. A biographical paper was written in 1982 by one of Josefa's great-grand-daughters named Terri Quintana which required that she interview her grandmother Celia Archuleta Quintana. She suggests that this branch of the family seems to have lived in Jemez Springs at least until the death of Basilio around 1916. Given data from Ms. Quintana's paper, it appears that Josefa may have died around 1918. Ms. Quintana does not give exact dates for the deaths of either Basilio or Josefa but simply says Josepha died two years after Basilio. Josefa and Basilio's children were Lydia, Francisco, Eloisa, Henry, Celia and Daniel. It is from this portion of the family that the Córdobas and Archuletas merge into one extended family of generally amiable cousins.

Interestingly, to my knowledge again, until recently all the Archuletas in Cuba were descendants of Josefa Córdoba's family. It is also interesting that it is members of this branch of the family that still hold titles to parts of the original Pascual Córdoba properties in Los Pinos.

For the most part, Pascual's brother Antonio's family stayed in the Gallina-Capulín area with three exceptions. Daniel, Isabel and Ignacita. Ignacita married Gabriel Montoya, Sr. and throughout her life was known as "Doña Cordova." Isabel married Mr. Aron Eichwald, who was a German Jew who immigrated to the United States in 1880. This family's version of their history is documented in a short monograph writted by Alex H. Eichwald, titled *Don Augustin, 1862–1927: An Immigrant, A Merchant and a Rancher*. Alex was one of Isabel and Don Augustin's sons.

Of the three children belonging to Antonio and Ignacita that made their homes in Cuba, only Daniel's two male children, Eddie and Elio would continue the Córdoba legacy from Antonio's side of the family in Cuba. The rest of Antonio's family, for the most part, live in the Gallina area and, although multitudinous, maintain close relationships with their cousins from the Pascual clan. Several generations later, most of us recognize our common heritage and we refer to each other as *primos* (cousins), knowing that in times of need we will be there as family.

A further reason that I have proposed that Señor Antonio de Córdoba was a Crypto-Jew or a converso has to do with the naming of the children following Mexico's independence from Spain in 1821.

Some may ask how someone named Pascual be a Crypto-Jew. Actually, *Pasqual* or *Pascua*, in Spanish, translates to Easter or to Passover. In Spanish, *Pascua* is derived from the Latin word *Pacha*, which is derived directly from the Hebrew word *Pe☐a☐*, which is the celebration of Passover. Yet the answer to the question about Pascual's name which makes a lot of sense to me is in Hordes book. "As we know, it was quite common for Iberian Jews to give Jewish Biblical names to their children before the expulsion and forced conversions in the late fifteenth century." Hordes goes on to say that following 1821, New Christians, *Conversos*, in their attempt to disguise their former ethnicity and assimilate into larger communities changed their naming practices. Instead, Crypto-Jews began giving their children names of popular Christian saints, such as Antonio, Francisco, José or Santiago. Among females, we find every girl's name was Maria followed by a name like Augustiana or Ana. Another option practiced was to have children baptized with classical names and names like Saturino (of Saturn) or even the name Santos. This obvious disguise, however, did not keep families from giving their children Hebrew Biblical names which were used at home but were not included in their official baptismal records.

Among the two Córdoba brothers' families, we see a change which for me confirms what Hordes is saying. In the generation following Protestant religious affiliation, we see three Pascuals: one in Francisco's family (a baby that did not live to adulthood), one in Julian's family and one in their cousin Donaciano's family. (Donaciano was one of Antonio's sons.) We also get three males named Elí, one Ruben and one Abrán. Abrán was passed down into the next generation which is interesting because this name seems to have been almost forbidden until after 1846. Hordes says, "a search of a comprehensive database *'Documentary Relations of the Southwest,'* revealed no males with the name Abrán (or Abrahán), Davíd, Isác, Leví, Rubén, Salamón, Samuél or Zacarías living in New Mexico between 1598 and 1821. Similarly, no citation could be found among the records for females named Debora, Esther, Lea, Raquel, Rebeca, Rut or Sara."

As I studied the baptismal records and the founding of the Capulín Church, it appears that in both of the Córdoba families, they picked Biblical names for the children of the next generation. Names such as Rachel, Gabriel, Esther, David, Pascual and Abrán, as I already mentioned an Abraham, son of Donaciano and Delfina Córdoba, there is also a Samuel Cordova.

Another interesting thing is that by 1933, Donaciano Isác Córdoba, son of Antonio, who had become a new Elder of the church, signed his middle name Isác, which I had not seen recorded before in the church register.

In concluding my hypothesis that our ancestor, Señor Antonio de Córdoba, was a Crypto-Jew fleeing the wrath and indignation of the Holy Office of the Inquisition. He did what many Crypto-Jews throughout Mexico had done after 1571. They fled to New Mexico, otherwise known as "The End of the Earth."

I do not expect my many cousins to agree with my premise. I, on the other hand, believe there is evidence enough and interesting research to show that the Córdobas who came to New Mexico and their offspring, which includes me, are true survivors of this interesting historical heritage. Albeit, given the amount of intermarriage between members of different religious backgrounds and native people which has occurred over the last three hundred years, my premise would be difficult to prove. Today, it would require many hours on "ancestry dot com" plus serious DNA testing. Who we are today would have very serious and different ramifications than it would have had during Señor Antonio de Córdoba's lifetime.

Among the most interesting patterns that emerged for me while working on this *Plática* is the apparent connection between Crypto-Jews and Presbyterians. To my knowledge, this is a unique component in New Mexico history. This, among our state's other exceptional qualities makes me very proud to be a native New Mexican.

"Los Primeros Protestants. " Three of the Cordova brothers (left to right): José Julian Cordova, Juan Francisco Cordova and José Marino Cordova, circa 1962.

Ruben Cordova at his beloved ranch with his favorite horse, "Branch"
and his faithful dog, "Chico," circa 1966.

Conflicting Expectations of Women's Roles
(Historical Society of New Mexico, April, 2016)

In April, 2016, The Historical Society of New Mexico held its annual conference in Farmington, New Mexico, in partnership with the San Juan County Historical Society. At this statewide conference, I was given the opportunity to speak about the conflicting expectations of women's roles that existed historically in northern New Mexico. Having been given this prestigious platform, I also addressed the issue of how it was that we got beyond these conflicts.

It is probable that these conflicts arose from an idealized notion of whet we in New Mexico refer to as *las hijas mujerotas y buenas mandadas*, the competent and obedient daughters. At the conference presentation, I focused primarily on the *mujerota* facet of this concept.

Unless you are a Spanish-speaker from northern New Mexico, it is likely you do not know what a *mujerota* is. In the first place, what makes this northern New Mexico regionalism interesting is the word *mujerota* itself. This word does not appear in any dictionary of Standard Modern Spanish. Secondly, even the late Ruben Cobos, in his life-long study of New Mexico and Southern Colorado Spanish doesn't quite translate the term as used here. He translates the term *mujerota* as "hard-working or brave female." Parenthetically, he says, "a lot of woman." What could that mean? These definitions do not depict the term, or the women, as we Northern New Mexicans use the term even today.

Historically, it appears as if, a long time ago, our local people amplified the word *mujer* (woman) to *mujerota* to fill their needs in describing their most competent, useful and able daughters and other similarly outstanding female members of their communities. These were women of such abilities and readiness to contribute their utmost efforts on behalf of their families' survival that they would rise to any occasion or task when it was needed.

How do I know of this? First of all, I experienced it. I am fortunate to be old enough — or should I say, "I am so old that..." — I witnessed this conflict in my own early childhood. I also had the good fortune to grow up in a world dominated by women. My mother was the oldest of six female siblings. I am only three years younger than my mother's youngest sister. These women, in addition to my grandmother and a multitude of great aunts and countless female cousins certainly shaped my perspective on at least three generations of female expectations. My grandfather and father as well, were usually working away from home much of the time and my mother's only male sibling left home before he was eighteen (and while I was very young).

These expectations of women's roles arose out of the harsh reality of a family's need to remain on their land and hopefully grow enough food crops and raise enough animals to survive from one year to the next. In most instances, the men in each family were working away from home, earning wages for those necessities that had to be purchased for cash. They herded sheep, worked in mines or did other manual labor nearby or as far away as Utah, Colorado or Wyoming. Young men rarely stayed at home beyond the age of about sixteen. Necessarily, what was to be done at home during these long absences had to be done by the women.

In the past, in Cuba and in neighboring settlements, a family that could truthfully claim to have *hijas mujerotas y buenas mandadas* (daughters who were competent and obedient) were looked upon with admiration and perhaps good-hearted envy. The family was considered blessed. Interestingly, in our early subsistence society, the expectations for these *hijas mujerotas* were no less challenging than those expected of their male siblings, if they had any. A lack of males could well determine the survival of an entire family. In the spring of 2016 a ninety-one-year old, life-long resident of Cuba died. This woman grew up with nine sisters and only two brothers. Unfortunately, one of the brothers was one of Cuba's World War II casualties, leaving a family with only one male heir.

While there were clearly defined responsibilities for both men and women, either might step in for the other when necessary. For example, men must have done their own cooking and laundry when they were away from home yet they must have looked forward to a good home-cooked meal and the company of their families when they returned. While they were gone, women did every task that would have been done by men.

True, the women did most of the cooking but cooking was only a fraction of the total range of jobs young women were expected to learn to do well. Women also did almost all of the gardening and sometimes supervised planting of acres of corn, wheat, beans and other crops.

They also continuously hauled water and did innumerable loads of laundry, by hand, a task no young man was ever expected to do at home. As a child, I watched my mother, my aunts and cousins perform every one of these labor-intensive jobs and many more, as they needed doing.

While doing the cooking and cleaning, women obviously also attended to the needs of babies and very young children. Among their many duties, women taught their young children how to behave, how to be respectful, and how to interact with other people, especially elderly adults. They also taught us all how to pray.

During haying season, it was not at all unusual for the young women to pitch hay onto wagons or into lofts that were several feet above their heads. Many of those women also rode horses as well as any of the men.

It was the young women who, under the watchful eye of well-trained older women, did all the mud plastering of *adobe* and *jacal* houses. As well, during those times the family's house was being expanded, women willingly helped make adobes in hope that the new addition could be closed in before the next winter.

True, while men collected material to make plaster and constructed scaffolding and ladders to reach the tops of walls. It was the women who climbed those ladders and scaffolds and plastered the walls of the local church and their own homes, generally every summer. Prior to corrugated metal roofs, water leaked in and stained the interior walls of houses every winter. So, women usually refinished all their interior walls each summer as well.

Separate from ordinary day-to-day, indoor and outdoor chores these women attended to, they were also expected to learn to sew, mend and do some kind of decorative stitchery such as embroidery or crocheting. In prior generations, the women also wove blankets for the entire family using upright looms and wool from their own sheep. A young woman who showed talent in these endeavors would be encouraged to become the family seamstress. This required a great deal of creativity because there were few, if any, resources, such as sufficient store-bought thread or an adequate amount of fabric to complete a project.

If a *mujerota* preferred baking to sewing, she might become the family's baker. This would become her job because she could bake the perfect *biscochitos* or the best yeast bread. The family would point out to their friends and neighbors that their daughter had the light hand necessary for baking leavened bread. Never mind that this potential artisan would also have to make the dozens of fresh *tortillas* required by the family each day. Naturally, these skills prepared the women who possessed them to be good candidates for marriage and motherhood.

An absolute curse for any family, particularly one with a gaggle of female children and few or no males was to have *una hija inútil* (a useless, fearful, incompetent daughter). Again, translation for the term *inútil*, as used locally, is difficult. What it implies is that the young woman simply did not measure up to the expected tasks. Furthermore, such a woman was a burden because she could not be counted on to do a task as thoroughly as required. Even a sickly daughter was not good to have around but could be tolerated. If there were daughters inclined to get sick often, someone else, one of the *mujerotas,* would have to pick up the slack.

Even this was not the most serious crisis for a family to endure while trying to survive; and it is survival that we are talking about. The worst possible situation was to have *una muchacha sin sentido* (a silly, brainless girl). This is the sort of young woman who would not milk the family's docile cow even though her udder was about to burst. The milk was badly needed by the household but she was afraid of the poor beast. Such a woman was also likely to let a newborn lamb or goat-kid freeze to death because she did not like the smell of the sheep or goats. These women were not only a burden but a liability to the entire family and were really looked down upon for their silliness. Since they developed few skills and were unreliable, they were not good candidates for marriage and would be a burden upon their families all their lives.

Given the obvious differences between *las hijas mujerotas, las hijas inútiles* and *las hijas sin sentido,* it is not difficult to understand why *las hijas mujerotas* were the recipients of high praise from all members of the adult community and how they became overachievers and perfectionists. These were the women other families sought to become the wives of their most eligible sons and the mothers of their legacies.

However, there were problems in this survival strategy. A serious conflict existed between what young women were expected to do in the harsh reality of living in a preindustrial agrarian society and the ideal traditional behavior deemed appropriate for all young women. These two behavior sets could hardly be more different.

On the one hand, these *mujerotas* were being praised for being the "go-getters" that could feed the pigs and milk the cow in the barnyard and, on the other hand, were expected to be well-groomed, obedient and otherwise "lady-like" while they were out in public. Mothers were constantly cautioning their talented daughters, *"No andan de adelantadas"* (don't be forward or assertive), or *"No vallan andar tontiando"* (above all, don't be silly or loud).

The message was that, while it was desirable and essential for these women to be able to perform at a high level of skill and, at times, substantial physical effort, at home it was not appropriate to do so beyond those boundaries. In cases where these women were really intelligent and even outspoken, many a candle must have been lit on their behalf to a patron saint that they would not embarrass the family by asking questions or expressing an opinion. Worse yet, perhaps she might show that she was brighter and more able than a young man who might be a prospective suitor.

There was a local mother who would harshly reprimand her inquisitive and outspoken daughter by calling her *la abogada* (the lawyer). This mother's greatest fear was that her daughter would put off any potential suitor with her outspoken opinions and never marry, thus becoming an embarrassment and a potential burden on her family.

Being competent and outspoken while attempting to be gentile and passive at the same time was not always easy. There could be severe consequences associated with trying to maintain both roles.

For example, there are many well-known cases throughout northern New Mexico where entire productive and successful estates and homesteads were lost by families lacking male influence or leadership following the death of a patriarch. When asked how these losses could be explained, the women of the family would respond that it would not have been appropriate for them to appear forward or assertive and stand up to a seemingly knowledgeable man. The tradition of being passive and "lady like" had been so ingrained in these women that they could not even speak out in behalf of their own welfare or their children's inheritance. We know that this happened many times because of the historical documentation that exists related to the land grabs that occurred following 1848 and during the late nineteenth century. Ultimately, the women from some of these families became destitute and totally dependent on others. In some cases, they were even displaced from their homes.

Contrary to the norm, those women who did assert themselves on behalf of themselves and their children were generally able to keep title to their properties and continued to be *mujerotas* in every sense of the word. In some cases, these women went so far as to remove their long lady-like skirts and put on men's trousers in order to move and work more efficiently. Of primary importance is that these women rose to the circumstances demanded of them without fear of the stigma of being thought of as *adelantadas* (forward and outspoken women).

In the past, the path these *mujerotas* could tread between praise and reprimand was very narrow. Yet, their contributions to their families' successes have become local legends. After all, it was these women's obvious competence that maintained the family's resources for the generations that followed.

I was just five years old in December of 1941, when World War II began. At that time, virtually all the men in our communities went into military service or went elsewhere to work in defense plants very far from home. By early 1942, Cuba, like many surrounding small communities in northern New Mexico, became a colony of women, children and a few elderly gentlemen, two priests and a dozen nuns and the Presbyterian minister. Without men in our community, I watched my mother, my grandmother and the other women around me take charge of their lives. One might say, "The Earth Shook," as we all know it did and from that moment on, our lives would never be the way they had been prior to this event, especially for women.

By the end of World War II, the *mujerotas* of our northern New Mexico hamlets had proven how competent they really were. During the war, many of them had learned to drive the few vehicles that were available and this allowed them basic and necessary mobility. More important, they had learned to manage their own money. Small as those government allotment checks may have been, our mothers and grandmothers were in charge of their own financial resources, in many cases, for the first time ever.

Above all, these women who had been left to their own devices during the war gave my generation the greatest gift of all, the permission to speak up in our own behalf. The results of these changes were astounding. We did become fearless lawyers, as well as social workers, educators and administrators, technicians of every sort and drivers of our own cars. We also learned through our mothers' examples how to manage our own financial resources as we earned our own livelihoods.

In the 1960s and 1970s, many of us became political activists as well as spokespersons against discrimination and the infringement of our civil rights. (Unfortunately, this is a job that is not yet complete.) Unlike our beloved grandmothers and great-grandmothers, young women today are not married off at the age of fourteen to some widower who needs a strong young woman to take care of his children after the death of his previous wife.

Today, our young women may choose who they want to marry or even whether they want to marry at all. Today's young women do not have to fear the stigma of becoming either a burden or an embarrassment to the "sacredness" of their family names.

I believe we owe these privileges to those *mujerotas* who came before us and who became our role models. It is because of these women's accomplishments that I am able to do the things I do today. It is my privilege to honor those hardworking, brave women of northern New Mexico who contributed so much with such few resources and such undying determination. This is why I want to tell their story!

Salaz wedding picture. This pitiful little child bride was only fourteen years old. Fortunately, she and Andres Salaz were happily married for forty-five years and had seven children. Circa 1928. Courtesy of Frances S. Oliva, their daughter.

148

The Graduate: Esther Cordova May, forty-six years after the wedding of her aunt Elzira, the fourteen-year-old, to Andres Salaz (previous picture).
Mills College, Oakland, California, 1974.

Four Generations of Teachers in the Epifanio Gutierrez Family
(Sandoval County Historical Society, 13 November, 2016)

Epifanio Gutierrez was born August 21, 1885, and attended school up to the eighth grade. According to family lore, when Epifanio completed this level of education he was asked if he would teach school the following term. Apparently, he had not only been the brightest student at the eighth-grade level but had also mastered English very well. According to the 1910 census, Epifanio is listed as being fifteen years old and an English speaker. The family does not know how many terms he taught. Recall that in the early twentieth century, New Mexico school terms varied between three and five winter months, depending on the district. What the family does remember about Don Epifanio is that he spoke very good English and was meticulous about his appearance. His image as as educated gentleman seems to have remained important to him all of his life.

The fact that Don Epifanio had learned English early and took pride in doing every job well would have qualified him not only to teach but also enabled him to participate competently in community improvement organizations such as the first Jemez Mountain Rural Electric Cooperative Board of Directors. As a rancher, he was also active in the New Mexico Wool Growers and Cattle Growers Associations. Ultimately, Don Epifanio did not become a professional teacher. Instead, he made his living by being a very well-informed rancher.

Don Epifanio had become an important role model for the Gutierrez family. He always expected hard work and determination along with dignity and pride from the members of his family. As a young parent, he must have also inspired two of his four children to become teachers. They were followed by four of his grandchildren and later, four of his great-grandchildren as professional teachers.

On Sunday, December 11, 1949, Epifanio and his wife Agapita endured an emotional but proud time in their life when the Cuba Health Center building was dedicated in memory of the nine young men from the Cuba and La Jara area who did not return from World War II. Their son, Anselmo Gutierrez, was among the nine whose names appeared on the plaque at the main entrance to the Cuba Health Center. Members of the family maintain the legacy of pausing to remember "Uncle Anselmo" as they approach the plaque at the entrance to the clinic.

Epifanio was a devout Catholic and a member of Santo Niño Church in La Jara, New Mexico. His strong faith sustained him through many difficult times. He faithfully served his church and lived to the age of one hundred and two years and seven months.

Rudolfo "Rudy" Gutierrez was born in November, 1915 to Agapita (Aragon) and Epifanio Gutierrez in La Jara, New Mexico. Rudy attended elementary school in La Jara. Approximately ten years after the opening of the Immaculate Conception Catholic School in Cuba, it received accreditation to teach high school. An accredited high school in Cuba gave Rudy the opportunity to attend high school under tremendous disadvantage due to the lack of transportation. Yet he was to become one of the first nine students to graduate from Cuba High School in 1936.

Since there was a shortage of teachers in those days, the state public school system began issuing Emergency Certificates to interested high school graduates. These "teachers" then continued their education by taking classes during summer vacation until they obtained their degrees in education. In 1937, Mr. Rudy Gutierrez began his teaching career with his Emergency Certificate at Vallecito de Los Pinos, a one-room school house located between Cuba and La Jara.

In August, 1938, Mr. Gutierrez married Lena Martinez. Since Lena's sister Ruben and her husband Trinidad Casaus lived next door to Los Pinos school house, Rudy and Lena moved in with the Casaus family. Rudy continued attending classes until he was drafted into the Army Air Corps in 1943 where he rose to the rank of Technical Sergeant. Upon his return from the service in 1946, Rudy attended the University of New Mexico and obtained his Bachelor of Science degree in Education through the G.I. Bill.

Following World War II, Mr. Rudy Gutierrez held many teaching positions in the Cuba area as well as being Principal of Cuba High School in the early to mid 1950s. Mr. Gutierrez was also Principal of Grants Middle School and Grants High School. He returned to the University of New Mexico where he earned a Master of Science degree in Education and became Superintendent of Jemez Mountain School District in Gallina, New Mexico. Mr. Gutierrez retired from education in the mid-1970s, following forty years of service as a second-generation teacher in New Mexico.

Among the many challenges he endured during his career was his wife Lena's disability following a series of strokes that eventually took her life in 1956. By then, there were six very young children to provide for while he was building his career. Rudy's six young children were greatly influenced by their aunt Angelita Gutierrez Olivas, Rudy's younger sister, as well as their grandmother Agapita, who were actively involved in raising the children.

Angelita had graduated from Cuba High School in 1937. Shortly after her graduation, she married William Olivas in 1938. After only one year of marriage, William became critically ill and died. Angelita was only nineteen years old and widowed. Like her brother before her, she soon began teaching with a state-issued Emergency Certificate while continuing her education during the summers.

Transportation, communication and housing were major factors involved in traveling to Albuquerque while trying to obtain certification. Eventually, several "teachers" managed to learn that there were host families in Albuquerque making room and board available for a reasonable amount of money for students attending summer school. Some of those families became Angelita's lifelong friends. She attended Saint Joseph's of the Rio Grande College in Albuquerque until she obtained her Bachelor of Science degree in Elementary Education.

One of Angelita's fondest memories while teaching was when she taught at the one-room school house in Vallecito de Los Pinos, where her brother had begun his career. Transportation was challenging due to the distance and lack of a road from her home in La Jara to the school. Riding a horse was her only transportation option. The winter months were the hardest but she was fortunate to have her very caring uncle, "Tio Kiko," Frank Gutierrez, living in Vallecito de Los Pinos. When it snowed a lot, he would meet her at the top of the hill where he had already cleared a path for her to get to school. He would then take her horse to his house and keep it there until she was ready to ride home in the evening. Sometimes she would stay the night, or even a few days, with her Uncle Frank and Aunt Lydia until the weather permitted her to return home.

Her next teaching assignment was at La Jara Elementary School where she taught for many years, until the school was closed down and the students were transported to Cuba Independent Schools. During her many years of teaching, she taught three generations of students from several families. Mrs. Olivas retired in the 1980s after forty-three years of service.

Angelita was always known as "Mrs. Olivas" and was highly respected in and around the community of La Jara and the surrounding area. She was very generous and not only taught school but took care of her elderly parents and her brother Rudy's children when he became a widower with six young children.

Rudy's oldest son, George William (Bill) Gutierrez and his oldest daughter, Rose (Gutierrez) Velarde eventually became the third generation of teachers in this family. Bill obtained a Bachelor of Science degree with a minor in Spanish from the University of New Mexico. He began his career at Aztec High School in Aztec, New Mexico. After a few years, his adventurous nature took him to study Spanish and Portuguese in Spain and Ecuador. He married Alicia Bustamante in 1968. They returned to New Mexico and he accepted a position teaching Spanish at Artesia High School in Artesia, New Mexico. They had two young daughters when Bill's career was tragically ended at the age of 36 when his friend took his life due to a jealous rage. This took a tremendous toll on Rudy and he was never the same after the loss of his eldest son.

Rudy's eldest daughter, Rose, obtained a Bachelor of Arts in Elementary Education with a minor in music from the University of New Mexico. Rose began her teaching career at Kit Carson Elementary School in Albuquerque. After teaching for four years, she married Randy Velarde and they started a family. After her three children were born, they moved to Cuba, New Mexico. She continued her career in the late 1970s at Cuba Elementary School and was the band leader at Cuba High School for a few years. She remained with the Cuba Independent School District until April 4, 1994, when she suffered a ruptured aneurism and passed away at the early age of 52.

After a few years, four of Rudy's grandchildren, Anna Marie (Casaus) Dusenbery, her brother Christopher Elias Casaus, their cousin Rosemary (Gutierrez) Dominguez and Rosemary's sister Ramona Lena Gutierrez followed in his footsteps to become the fourth generation of Gutierrez family teachers. (Anna Marie and Christopher are the children of Judy Ann (Gutierrez) Casaus and Abenicio Casaus. Rosemary and her sister Ramona are the daughters of Rudy Gutierrez, Jr. and Annie Gutierrez.)

Anna Marie (Casaus) Dusenbery began her career in 1990 after obtaining a Bachelor of Science degree in Secondary Education at New Mexico State University in Las Cruces. She began teaching sixth grade at Immaculate Conception School in Cuba, New Mexico. She later taught English at Las Cruces High School for three years and then accepted a position with the Farmington (New Mexico) Municipal Schools for five years. In 1995, she married Jimmy Dusenbery and started a family. Before her two daughters were in school, Anna Marie began teaching English classes part-time at San Juan College in Farmington where she remained for eight years. Then, in 2004, she received a Master of Arts degree in Secondary Education from the University of New Mexico. She has been teaching at Vista Nueva High School, an alternative school, in Aztec, New Mexico, for the past seven years.

Christopher (Chris E.) Casaus received a Bachelor of Science degree in Secondary Education in 1993 from New Mexico State University. Chris has been teaching math and science at Escalante High School in the Chama Valley (New Mexico) School District since 1994. He has also been the district Computer Tech for most of the 22 years he has been with the Chama Valley Schools. His "Auntie Rosie" (Rose Velarde) unknowingly passed the teaching torch to Chris when he took over her classes as a permanent substitute for the remainder of the school year after her death in April, 1994.

Rosemary (Gutierrez) Dominguez obtained a Bachelor of Music degree in Elementary Education at the University of New Mexico. In 2005, she obtained a Masters degree in Business Administration and began her career with the Albuquerque Public Schools system where she teaches in the Fine Arts Department. She has been with the Albuquerque Public School system for fifteen years.

Ramona Lena Gutierrez received her Bachelor of Art Education degree and Master of Arts degree in Elementary Education in 2013 and has been with the Albuquerque Public School Fine Arts Department since 2014.

The legacy of Don Epifanio Gutierrez's success as a family that has, to date, contributed so greatly "unto the fourth generation" of dedicated educators is truly admirable. Despite the horrific losses of immediate family members, they have overcome their losses and have risen to meet the expectations he exemplified: "hard work and determination, along with dignity and pride."

I extend my loving gratitude to Judy Gutierrez Casaus, who contributed greatly to this chapter. She also participated in a presentation by three local individuals about the contributions of the "Early Pioneer Teachers of Northern New Mexico." Her original script, along with a photographic display was submitted to the Sandoval County Historical Society Archive on November 13, 2016.

Don Epifanio Gutierrez (1885–1987) surrounded by his great-grandchildren.

Rudolfo (Rudy) Gutierrez, one of
the first nine graduates from Cuba
Convent's High School, 1936.

Angelita Gutierrez Olivas, 1918–2006, sister of Rudy Gutierrez.
She was a dedicated teacher in the Cuba area for forty-three years.

George William (Bill) Gutierrez, 1939–1975. Son of Rudy and Lena Martinez Gutierrez.

Rose Ramona Gutierrez Velarde,
1940–1994. Daughter of Rudy
and Lena Gutierrez.

Anna Marie Casaus Dusenbery.
Daughter of Abenicio and Judy
(Gutierrez) Casaus and granddaughter
of Rudy and Lena Gutierrez.

Chris E. Casaus, son of Abenicio and Judy (Gutierrez) Casaus, brother of Anna Marie.
They are great grandchildren of Epifanio Gutierrez.

All photographs in this chapter were provided by Judy Gutierrez Casaus.
No photographs were available of Ramona Lena Gutierrez or Rosemary Gutierrez
Dominguez, daughters of Rudy Gutierrez, Jr. and great-grandchildren of Epifanio Gutierrez.

Leonor Lucero Cordova, Pioneer Teacher
(Sandoval County Historical Society, 13 November, 2016)

Leonor was born April 11, 1887 in Cuba, New Mexico. (This was the same year the United States Postal Service established a post office in what had been called Nacimiento. The name was changed to Cuba.) Leonor was the oldest of six daughters born to Manuel Reyes Lucero and Teresita Montoya Lucero.

Manuel Reyes was a teacher and apparently devoted a lot of his effort to his daughter Leonor, perhaps toward the goal that she, in time, would become a certified teacher herself. This woman was literate and bilingual in English and Spanish, a mastery that is well documented in her correspondence which still exists among the family's papers and photographs. Yet, I have no documentation of Leonor or her sisters ever attending school other than their father's one-room school.

Until very recently, I knew very little about this remarkable woman, even though she had been my father's mother. My father, Ruben Cordova, was only eight years old when Leonor died in the flu epidemic of 1918. My father never talked about his mother, so I grew up only knowing that she had died in the flu epidemic like so many other people around here.

In the spring of 2016, while in contact with one of my father's nieces, Frances Oliva, I mentioned to her how valuable our great-grand-father Manuel Reyes' journals had been to me in documenting events for my writing. Suddenly, my cousin said to me, "Oh, my mother (my father's sister) left me a little book that belonged to our grandmother Leonor." Then she apologetically said, "it is hand-written in Spanish and I've never read it." Not ever having heard of this little book, I asked her to send me a copy which she happily agreed to do. A short time after this conversation, I received copies of sixteen loose little pages of what my grandmother had titled her *"Memoránda."* It is a treasure trove of information about how, in her short life, she had dedicated herself to becoming a certified teacher and, in between school terms, a post mistress in Gallina, New Mexico. Gallina was where she and her husband, Juan Francisco Cordova lived and, with great effort, had their family in the early twentieth century.

Leonor was sixteen years old in 1903, when she married my grandfather, Juan Francisco, a man who was ten years older than she. Between 1905, when Leonor's first child was born and 1916 when she had her last child, Terecita, she had given birth to six children. Only three of these children survived to adulthood. When Leonor died on December 17, 1918, at the age of thirty-one, her youngest child was just two years old. Elzira became five in August of that year and my father, Ruben, was only eight years old. There had been another child born between them that did not survive. Between June, 1905 and May, 1916 when Terecita was born, Leonor had borne six children, held a job as post mistress in Gallina and had been teaching in various places.

Leonor's first teaching assignment was in what she called *la escuela publica* (the public school) in Capulín, a settlement that used to be located several miles from Gallina, on the way to Coyote. The school term was only four months long and during the winter months. Keep in mind that she had given birth to her first baby in June of 1905. This child apparently did not survive infancy and there is no mention of when she died. Living in Gallina and teaching in Capulín must have meant that she would have had to travel on horseback between the two communities or live with a family in Capulín during the week, which many teachers of that time had to do.

Being bilingual, young and highly literate, she was named post mistress in Gallina on July 18, 1907. According to Robert Julyan, this post office was established in 1888 as Jacquez Post Office, then changed to Gallina in 1890. This was the post office Leonor was appointed to manage. At that time, she would also have been pregnant with her second child, born on January 2, 1908 in Cuba. She was only twenty years old. Very likely, that child was born at her parents' home. This second child, named Pascual, after Francisco's father, apparently did not survive infancy either and again, there is no record of his death.

In August of 1908, Leonor states in her *Memoránda* that she went to take her first examination toward becoming certified as a teacher. That winter term, she taught in Gallina for the four-month term, presumably along with her post office responsibilities. Four to five months was the common school term in New Mexico at that time. Leonor wrote that she returned to Española for four weeks to attend what she called *El Instituto Normal* (the teachers' institute). It appears that these *Institutos* were summer training seminars for people who had the desire to teach in rural school districts. Certification was dependent on passing a state-administered examination. Leonor took and passed the exams and was certified September 5, 1909. She was very precise in documenting every date, place and duration of these exams which allowed her to teach.

In 1908, she also left her job as post mistress in Gallina and came to Cuba to teach from October, 1909 until March, 1910. She would have been very pregnant by the end of this term since her third child, my father, was born on May 7, 1910. Incidentally, my father and I were born in the same house on what was then land belonging to Leonor's father.

What happens next leaves some questions unanswered in the *Memoránda*. She now has this baby and is very likely living with her family here in Cuba. My father's birth certificate indicates that he was born in Cuba. Yet, in July, 1910, she states that she attended *El Instituto Normal* in Bernallilo. Keep in mind that the baby is only two months old when Leonor left for Bernallilo for four weeks. Once again, she passed the exams and was certified to teach for five months in La Jara, located between Cuba and Gallina. There is no mention of who is taking care of the baby or what she would do with the child while she taught in La Jara. La Jara is no more than ten miles from Cuba but she would have had to spend some time living there while teaching in the winter. I have to assume the baby was left with her family and cared for by her parents and younger sisters. Furthermore, in those days, mothers breast-fed their babies for at least a year. Again, I have to assume my father was bottle fed from a very young age but, unlike his two previous siblings, he survived. All this time, Leonor was striving to succeed at what appears, even by today's standards, at tremendous sacrifice to her and her family. At this point in Leonor's accounts of her life, one must ask what the motivation was for this woman to pursue this lifestyle with such intensity. Part of the answer to this question may relate to entries about how her husband, Francisco, was earning a living when they married and what he did during the early part of their married life. By 1911, Leonor was apparently back in Gallina because in July she went back to Española for recertification. That year, she again taught in Capulín and was pregnant with her fourth child. Capulín seems to have been her last teaching assignment since her baby was born in May, 1912 and she stated that she went back to being a post mistress in Gallina. There is documentation that in 1915 she was still post mistress in Gallina and apparently held that position while she had two more children and until her untimely death in 1918.

Back to the motivation for Leonor to remain teaching and staying certified, there are several journal entries related to her husband Francisco's "occupation" and his seeming inability to provide adequately for his family. The first reference has to do with his employment at the time of their marriage. Again, in Leonor's precise style, she stated that on July 20, 1903, she and Francisco were united in marriage in Park View, New Mexico (originally known as Los Ojos). Between 1877 and 1972, this community was known as Park View because of a post office by that name having been established there. This community is in Rio Arriba county, north of the town of Tierra Amarilla and south of Chama. It is also located near a community named Edith, which does not exist anymore, where sawmills were operated in one of the heavily forested areas of northern New Mexico. Leonor stated that they lived in Edith shortly after their marriage where her husband worked *solamente* (only) at the sawmill. She then says that on November 1, 1904, they came to Los Pinos, basically Francisco's family's homestead in the foothills north of Cuba. She then said that in that year Francisco planted his mother's property and was rewarded with a good harvest. I have no record of when Francisco's father, Pascual Cordova, died. His death may have been the reason Francisco left his job in Edith and returned home "to plant his mother's property." What Leonor does document very clearly is that on November 1, 1905, one year to the day after arriving, they moved back to Gallina and that winter she was teaching in Capulín. She also stated that they moved into their own house, which was apparently built by Francisco on *Domocilio Publico* (public domain). (According to Webster's New World Dictionary, public domain is "(1) public lands, (2) the condition of being free from copyright or patent and hence, open to use by anyone." Francisco apparently took advantage of this and started cultivating the land immediately after building a house there.

Recall that 1911 was when Leonor went back to being post mistress. It also seems to be the last year she taught. That year seems significant for another reason. In the journal, there is an entry where she said, "on February 5, 1911, Francisco made a trip to the state of Arizona, returning May 12, 1911. No reason is given for this journey. She simply followed by saying that upon his return, Francisco immediately started laboring on his land again. Leonor would have been post mistress as well as taking care of her then one-year-old son (my father) while Francisco was gone. By May of 1912, Ruben would have been exactly two years old when his sister Eloyda was born. This child survived probably for a few years because there is a picture of her as a toddler. Again, there is no mention of how or when she died. Leonor would go on to have two more children, Elzira, born in Gallina in 1914 and Teresita, born in Cuba in 1916.

So once more, what motivated this woman? Given her own documentation of her careers, it appears that she was the primary bread winner of an ever-growing family. This, in my opinion, translates to money, which was what kept this woman going to school, teaching for four or five months in the depth of winter and keeping her government job at the post office. These jobs paid real money in the rural, agrarian society in which they lived. It is obvious, given her accomplishments, that she had the skillset and was prepared to endure the hardships the jobs demanded of her in order to earn the few dollars she was paid as a teacher and post mistress. All the time, her husband was cultivating and harvesting crops in order to provide food for their family.

Personally, having read these sixteen loose little pieces of my grandmother's *Memoránda* has been painful. What is painful is that it took eighty years for me to learn what this exceptionally strong woman went through. It is excruciating for me even now as I write about her untold accomplishments, her professionalism and her obvious intellect. Furthermore, I feel a deeper obligation to tell her story.

Most importantly, I can now understand my father far better than I did before I learned what he must have suffered in his mother's absence. I also firmly believe that my father never got over his mother's death. My reasons for saying this are, as I stated earlier, my father never, ever told me anything about my grandmother while I was growing up. Furthermore, several years ago, I was preparing some memorabilia to donate to the Menaul Historical Library and I came across the 1931 *Sandstorm*. This was the yearbook of my father's graduating class at Menaul. I started looking through it and discovered that, in his senior year of high school, my father had won first prize in the writing of poetry. The title of his poem is "My Mother." The entire poem follows:

My Mother

> In lonely solitude, I often remember you
> And the many things you did for me.
> And how little did I ever do for thee.
> Often have I asked that I be, too,
> Where thou art, and do what ere you do.
> Mother, my beloved mother, how happy we could be
> If again you could sing and talk to me
> As once I was sung to sleep by you.
> The years have passed but I remember still
> When but a child you took me in your arms,
> Protected me from dangers and all harms.
> The time has flown and time is flying still
> But I remember now and always will
> My mother with her love and graceful charms.

> —Ruben Cordova, 1931

Another reason that I believe my father never got over the death of his mother relates to what my mother told me had been his last request before his own death. There was, in my parents' home, a traditional, probably ten-by twelve-inch oval-framed photograph of Leonor that I remember vividly. I returned to Cuba from California for my father's funeral and to assist my mother with the arrangements and what happened after his sudden death, on what would have been his mother's eighty-first birthday, April 11, 1978. Several days after the funeral, I noticed that grandmother Leonor's photograph was not in its usual place. I asked my mother where the photograph was and she told me that my father had asked her to put that photograph in his coffin when he died. He would never again be left without his beloved mother, Leonor Lucero Cordova.

Leonor Lucero Cordova, oldest of a family of six female children.

Manuel Reyes Lucero and his wife Teresita Montoya Lucero, parents of Leonor Lucero. Manuel Reyes was born in 1862 in the settlement of Conejos in the San Luis Valley in what would later become the state of Colorado.

A Dedication in Response to an Honor
(Graduation Address, Cuba High School, 18 May, 2013)

In early April, 2013, I received a telephone call from a young woman who identified herself as Carly Thomas, a senior at Cuba High School, and president of the senior class.

I immediately recognized who this bright, ambitious young woman was. I had known Carly since she was an infant. Furthermore, her late mother, Brandy Thomas, had been one of my very promising students. As we spoke, Carly told me the reason she was calling was in behalf of the senior class who wanted me to deliver their commencement address on May 18, 2013.

By then, I had been retired from teaching at Cuba Schools for seventeen years. I was seventy-seven years old. As Carly and I talked, I thought, what can I possibly say to a modern "hip" generation of bright, computer-era students that would be meaningful and that they would re-member. It dawned on me that many of these students were the children of my most admirable former students. Others, like Adrian Cordova, Nicolas Crespin, Kaylin Lovato and Sara Archuleta were actually related to me. I accepted the invitation.

A few days later, I received their acknowledgement in the form of a beautiful card with the following touching message. How could I not give this class my utmost effort?

> *Class of 2013*
> *The Graduating class of 2013 cordially*
> *Invites you to attend our Graduation Ceremonies on*
> *May 18, 2013*
> *10:00 a.m. in the High School Gymnasium.*

We would like to bestow on you,
Our gratitude and appreciation for honoring us
As our Guest Speaker!!
You are a Pillar in our community and a role-model
For our Graduating Class!

A message to the readers: I was told before I addressed this class of graduates that the majority of the class were Native American, more specifically, members of the Navajo Tribe. Although known as Navajo, they refer to themselves as *Diné*, meaning "The People," which is how they prefer to be known. I use the term *Diné* in my speech out of courtesy to them. I also use the term *Nakai*, which means Hispanic, or Spanish speakers in general. I am known to them as *Nakai* as they are known to me as *Diné*.

To the 2013 Graduating Class of
Cuba High School
May 18, 2013

Good morning ladies and gentlemen! I am Esther Cordova May and I am deeply honored to have been invited to address this very special class of graduates.

You are a special class to me because you were born around the time that I retired from teaching and, over the years, many of your parents, your aunts and uncles have been my students.

That could make me your <u>grandmother!</u>

Others of you are my cousins. Thus, I could be your <u>cousin-grand-mother.</u> For the *Diné* graduates, if you like, I can be your *Nakai* grandmother.

Given all the excitement of today's ceremony and all the parties and dances you will have attended, hopefully some of you will remember something of what I am going to say to you today.

It has been written that today, when you walk out the same door you came in this morning, you will be high school graduates. The very diploma that you are anxiously waiting to receive today will declare that fact. Thereby, you will no longer be part of Cuba High School. While you sit here awaiting your diploma, your status will have changed.

You will have been transformed into young adults and the whole world, the world beyond Cuba, the world beyond the safe shelter of your family, will now have different expectations of you.

In part, I am here today to announce to you that your BABYHOOD is over!

As you each grow into adulthood, you must find your own truths. You must also learn to see yourselves as other people see you.

However, I am also here to try to prepare you for some of the SHOCK you will experience in that great beyond called REALITY: not virtual reality but reality in the modern world!

As I drafted this message, I seriously considered having a small mirror given to each of you as you marched into the ceremony.

One reason for the mirror would have been for you to see how beautiful and proud you look today.

The other reason I would have you look into the mirrors is to see for yourselves who you are and to find out how comfortable you are with whom you see in that mirror.

The big questions that nag at me in relation to you, my would-be grandchildren, are:

> Do you know who you are?
>
> Are you proud of who you are?
>
> Do you know the wonderful history we share?

This is a history and a legacy that will follow you no matter how far you may move away from our Sacred Mountains or how many degrees and honors you receive throughout your careers. You will still be the same person in the mirror.

Given my many years of experience with young people, I can assure you success will be achieved sooner and more completely by those of you who have looked into the mirror knowing proudly and comfortably who you are.

If so, you are standing on firm ground and NO ONE can take that away from you. Nor can anyone outside yourself define who you are.

There are going to be many instances when you will be minding your own business and some "nobody," whether well-meaning or otherwise, will ask, innocently perhaps;" "What are you anyway?" NOT "Who are you?" but What are you?"

It is my deepest and most sincere hope that when this happens each and every one of you will be prepared to answer proudly and without hesitating WHO you are and not WHAT you are.

If you respond to such a question that you are from New Mexico, you will be shocked to realize that there are still people in the United States, after one hundred and one years, who don't realize New Mexico is a state and will tell you what a lovely country you are from and what a great time they had in Acapulco!

Others will attempt to define who you are by the names they call you. Depending on where you are in the country, you may be called a "greaser," a "spick," "Mex," "Chief," a "Tío Taco," "Smokey," "squaw" or the converse of that: "a beautiful Indian princess."

Some will attempt to define you by pretending they can't pronounce your names and will attach to you a name that is easy for them to use, whether or not this name has anything to do with you, your family's legacy, history or culture.

You can accept these insults quietly, you can choose to get angry and resentful or you can be who you are and become better than anyone else at everything you do.

You are going to have to live and work among many different kinds of people but do so on your own terms regardless of what other people call you without compromising who you are.

The racism, the insensitivities, the indignities and the prejudices that you will encounter are not easy to ignore or tolerate. These are painful, hurtful experiences. This is why you must leave here today determined to foster a legacy that you will be a proud and honorable person.

By honorable, I mean a person that has no need to lie or cheat. A proud and honorable person prospers on his or her own merits, not at the expense of others.

Unfortunately, you may find this task difficult to maintain in today's world. But when you have doubts about who you really are, look into the biggest mirror you can find, stand tall and proud and recall how splendid and self-assured you feel today.

Remember each of you is the inheritor of all you have learned from your elders and the people around you.

You are the next generation of your cultural heritage and this is what makes US, *you and me, who* we are, not *what* we are.

As your "honorary grandmother," I stand here today exceedingly proud of you and as you march out into that great beyond, diploma in hand, try to retain this "Bright and Shining Moment" in May, 2013.

I leave you with these few words by Native American writer Linda Hogan given to me by my friend Connie Aguilar.

> "Walking I am listening to a deeper way.
> Suddenly all my ancestors are behind me.
> Be still, they say, watch and listen.
> You are the result of the LOVE of thousands."

You can't ask for much more than that, can you?
Thank you and congratulations to each and every one of you!

Dedication

In return for the honor you bestowed on me, I now dedicate this book to the Cuba High School Class of 2013. It is my hope that you have succeeded in all that you have attempted to do since we last shared that "Bright and Shining Moment" on May 18, 2013, your graduation day!

Post Script: We mourn the untimely death on July 18, 2013, of Kathan T. Bridge, a graduating member of this promising class. Postscript published with the consent of Dustin and Oralia Bridge, Kathan's parents.

2013 Senior Class

Adams, Nikivar R

Albert, Titus T

Angus-Estrada, Jessica C*

Archuleta, Sarah M*

Arellano, Erica V

Bridge, Kathan T

Castillo, Cristen D

Castillo, Dominique M

Castillo, Doramie S

Castillo, Nicole L

Castillo, Sammy

Castillo, Tiffany

Castillo, Trisha J

Castillo, Waylon M

Castillo, Will W

Cayaditto, Kristain L*

Charley, Johnson

Chavez, Cassandra

Litfin, Stephan D*

Lopez, Mareintina M

Lovato, Kaylin*

Lucero, Joshua A

Martin, Claudia

Morgan, Ember L

Pena, Katrina C*

Pinto, Lulonda*

Pinto, Marcus

Pinto, Taryl D

Platero, Ashley L

Sala, Deidrick

Salaz, Zachary*

Sam, Alexzandria E

Sam, Natasha R

Sam, Wilcinda

Sanchez, Josiah M*

Thomas, Carly M*

Cuba High School Graduates, 2013.

Chiquito, Ashlyn R

Cordova, Adrian R*

Crespin, Nicolas*

Diaz, Amaris B

Elliot, William E

Francisco, Benny

Francisco, Joshua

Gutierrez, Trini S*

Herrera, Alycia

Herrera, Jaeson A

Jim, Terrence C

Thomas, Hannah L*

Thomas, Tenisha K*

Tijerina, Adam F

Toledo, Jagger L

Toledo, Joshua-Joe

Trujillo, Mildred

Trujillo, Tierra M

Tsosie, Chenoah

Tsosie, Larson

Vazquez, Viviana

Yazzie, Ashley*

* National Honor Society Members

Cuba High School Graduates, 2013, continued.

EPILOGUE

Initially, my plan was to have the book form of the *Pláticas* articles done before I was eighty years old. Due to family medical issues, requests for presentations to local groups of students and inertia on my part, I somehow became eighty years old. Then there was the invitation to address the Historical Society of New Mexico in 2016. This was a presentation I could not decline. Preparation for this event was not something I had calculated when I agreed to be a part of this annual event. The experience was good and the topic of my presentation, *Conflicting Expectations of Women's Roles,* was a conversation I deeply wanted to have with a larger audience than I had here. Furthermore, I had the added opportunity to include the entire text in this book.

According to May Sarton, "The wonderful thing about conversation is that it stimulates one to new insights." I have been rewarded greatly by every one of the conversations in this book. It is now my heartfelt hope that the *pláticas* shared here will stimulate new insights for every reader. It is also my hope that especially among "my would-be grandchildren" (members of the graduating class of 2013, the youth of this community), that this will inspire your generation to participate in creating a better world through truly honorable and more inclusive strategies.

The challenges being faced in the twenty-first century by all of us have already surpassed the issues addressed in the conversations in this small collection. Valid as our concerns might have been, what lies ahead will require dreamers that can dream beyond the stratosphere. Again, it is my hope that among such dreamers, thinkers and inventors, there will be those of you who have gleaned insights from the conversations we have shared.

The problems the world faces today are enormous compared to those of previous generations. The challenges related to climate change alone will require choices that would outdo the likes of grandma Leonor Lucero Cordova, or the *Mujerotas* who put on men's trousers when they had to, in order to prevail over long-held traditions, leap over hurdles they had not been prepared for when World War II came to them.

Barring dramatic changes in governmental politics, I believe that in the very near future, our once prosperous and generous society will be faced with the actual decision of the survival of millions of truly indigent people. This would include children, the vulnerable disabled population, such as our own Juan Rafael or Vincent May and a large segment of elderly people. They might have no access to health care or even basic care as was the case in the early twentieth century in New Mexico. As I ponder such a future, I am counting on new insights brought upon by sincere conversations and negotiations to accomplish these daunting tasks. I am also concerned about the perpetuation of our long history of caring about the welfare of the many as opposed to the privileges of the few.

I would also like to think that I could confidently predict that no one we have known, loved or shared experiences with in this community will be left unaware that they are remembered as having had a place of belonging in such a place as Cuba, New Mexico. This undertaking can only be achieved through sincere conversations among people like ourselves and those of the stalwart people who came before us and taught us the art of meaningful *pláticas*.

Con todo cariño y amistad.
(With affection and friendship)

Esther V. Cordova May

Bibliography

Anaya, Rudolfo. *Bless Me, Última.* Berkeley, California: TQS, 1972.

Anonymous. *Nueva Novena dedicada al Milagrosisimo Niño de Nuestra Señora de Atocha.* Mexico City: Antigua Imprenta de Murguia, no date.

Anonymous. *Ramillete de Divinas Flores, Nueva Edición Aumentada.* Paris: Charles Bouret(?), 1912.

Anonymous. *The Catholic's Guide: A Manual of Devotion for the Use of Catholics.* Revised by a Jesuit Father. New York: The Regina Press, 1924.

Baez, Joan (ed.). *From Every Stage.* Hollywood, California: Alamo Publications, 1976.

Baker, Pauline. *Español Para Los Hispanos.* Skokie, Illinois: National Textbook Company, 1966.

Carillo Dueñas, Manuel. *Madre Santisima del Rosario de Talpa.* Guadalajara, Mexico: Linotipográficos Jalisco (printer), 1961.

Carson, Chris, Sponsor. *The Ram: Cuba High School Year Book, 1995–1996.* Eden Prairie, Minnesota: Life Touch Publishing, 1996.

Chávez, Fray Angélico, *Origins of New Mexico Families.* Santa Fé, New Mexico: The Historical Society of New Mexico, 1954.

Chávez, Fray Angélico. *But Time and Chance: The Story of Padre Martinez of Taos, 1793–1867.* Santa Fé, New Mexico: Sunstone Press, 1981.

Cobos, Ruben. *A Dictionary of New Mexico and Southern Colorado Spanish.* Rev. and exp. Santa Fé, New Mexico: Museum of New Mexico Press, 2003.

Cohen, Herbert J., ed. *Page One: Major events, 1920–1983 as presented in the New York Times, Rev. and Updated.* New York: Times Books, 1983.

Cordova, Leonor Lucero. "Memoránda." (Personal diary, 1903–1912.) Gallina, New Mexico. [1912].

De Lavalle, J. A. *Reposo en Dios: Devocionario que contiene el Santo Sacraficio de la Misa.* Winterberg, Czechoslovakia: J. Steinbrener, 1911.

Deck, Rev. E. M. *Catechism for Beginners.* Buffalo, New York: Rauch and Stoeckl Printing Co., 1930.

Dickinson, Emily. *Collected Poems of Emily Dickinson.* New York: Avenel Books, 1982.

Eichwald, Alex H. *Don Augustin, 1862–1927: An Immigrant, a Merchant, and a Rancher.* Self published, no date.

Flynn, Kathryn A. (compiler, ed.). *New Mexico Blue Book, 2005–2006.* Albuquerque, New Mexico: LithExcel, 2006.

García, Nasario. *Más Antes: Hispanic Folklore of the Rio Puerco Valley.* Santa Fé, New Mexico: Museum of New Mexico Press, 1997.

Gordon, Lesley. *A Country Herbal.* New York: Mayflower Books, 1980.

Hordes, Stanley M. *To the End of the Earth: A History of the Crypto-Jews of New Mexico.* New York: Columbia University Press, 2005.

Immaculate Conception Convent School. *Convent School Journal, 1916–1980.* Cuba, New Mexico: Immaculate Conception Convent, unpublished manuscript, no date.

Jimenez, Juan Ramon. "El Viaje Definitivo," in *Literatura del Siglo XX: Antologia Selecta,* edited by Margarita U. DaCal and Ernesto G. DaCal. New York: Holt, Rinehart and Winston, 1954.

Jones, Jr., Oakah L. *Los Paisonos: Spanish Settlements of the Northern Frontier of New Spain.* Norman, Oklahoma: University of Oklahoma Press, 1979.

Judson, Sylvia Shaw. *The Quiet Eye.* 3rd. ed. Chicago, Illinois: Regnery Gateway Inc., 1982.

Julyan, Robert. *The Place Names of New Mexico.* Rev. ed. Albuquerque, New Mexico: University of New Mexico Press, 1998.

Lapesa, Rafael. *Historia de la Lengua Español, Septima Edición.* Madrid: Escelicer S.A., 1968.

Market House Books Ltd. (Eds.), *Oxford Encyclopedia of World History.* New York: Oxford University Press, 1998.

Laumbach, Rudy (editor-in-chief). *Sandstorm: Menaul High School Yearbook, 1931 edition.* Fort Worth, Texas: Southwest Engraving Co., College Annual Engravers, 1931.

McLuhan, T. C. *Dream Tracks: The Railroads and the American Indians, 1890–1930.* New York: Harry N. Abrams, Inc., 1975?

Meyer, Michael, and William L. Sherman. *The Course of Mexican History.* New York: Oxford University Press, 1983.

Montoya, Esther L., (ed.) *The Ram: Cuba High School Year Book, Vol. 12.* Wolfe City, Texas: Henington Publishing Co., 1964.

Moore, Michael. *Los Remedios: Traditional Herbal Remedies of the Southwest.* Santa Fé, New Mexico: Museum of New Mexico Press, 1990.

Morales, Janine, (ed.) *The Ram: Cuba High School Year Book, 1997–1998.* Eden Prairie, Minnesota: Life Touch Publishing, 1998.

Morris, Richard B. and Jeffrey B. Morris. *Encyclopedia of American History, 6th Ed.* New York: Harper and Row, 1982.

National Textbook Co. (eds). *VOX: New College Spanish and English Dictionary.* Chicago, Illinois: National Textbook Co. 1984.

New Mexico Land Resources Association. *Land Resources of New Mexico.* Publisher uncertain, 1957.

Olibama López Tushar. *The People of "El Valle:" A History of the Colonials in the San Luis Valley.* Denver: Olibama López Tushar, 1975.

Quintana, Terrie. "Student Interview with Celia Quintana." (Class assignment, University of New Mexico, Albuquerque, New Mexico, 1982).

Real Academia Española (eds.). *Diccionario de la Lengua Española.*Madrid, *Espasa-Calpe, S.A.,*1970.

Roberts, Susan A. and Calvin A. Roberts. *A History of New Mexico.* Albuquerque, New Mexico: University of New Mexico Press, 1986.

Rulfo, Juan. "Luvinia," in *Cinco Maestros: Cuentos modernos de Hispanoamérica,* edited by Alexander Coleman. New York: Harcourt, Brace & World, Inc. 1969.

Sarton, May. *As We Are Now.* New York: W. W. Norton & Company, 1973.

Sarton, May. *Coming Into Eighty: New Poems.* New York: W. W. Norton & Company, 1994.

Sarton, May. *The House By The Sea: A Journal.* New York: W. W. Norton & Company, 1977.

Sarton, May. *The Small Room.* New York: W. W. Norton & Company, 1961.

Schackel, Sandra. *Social Housekeepers: Women Shaping Public Policy in New Mexico, 1920–1940.* Albuquerque, New Mexico: University of New Mexico Press, 1992.

Session of the Capulín Spanish Presbyterian Church. *Minutes of the Session, 1887–1940.* Capulín, New Mexico: unpublished manuscript, [1940].

Session of the Cuba Spanish Presbyterian Church. *Minutes of the Session, 1940–77.* Cuba, New Mexico: unpublished manuscript, [1977].

Session of the San José Spanish Presbyterian Church. *Minutes of the Session, 1913–1927.* Regina, New Mexico: unpublished manuscript, [1927].

Silko, Leslie Marmon. *Gardens in the Dunes.* New York: Simon and Schuster, 1999.

Silko, Leslie Marmon. *Laguna Woman, 2nd. Ed.* Tucson, Arizona: Flood Plain Press, 1994.

Silko, Leslie Marmon. *Sacred Water, 2nd, Ed.* Tucson, Arizona: Floodplain Press, 1998.

Sisneros, Francisco and Joe H. Torres. *Nobres: Nombres de Pila in Nuevo Mexico.* Bernalillo, New Mexico: Las Campanas Publications, 1982.

Smith, William, revised by Rev. F. N. and M. A. Peloubet. *A Dictionary of the Bible.* Philadelphia, Pennsylvania: John C. Winston Co., 1884.

Swadesh, Frances Leon. *Los Primeros Pobladores: Hispanic Americans of the Ute Frontier.* Notre Dame, Indiana: University of Notre Dame Press, 1974.

Un Padre Redentorista. *Id Á Jesús: Librito Piadoso para la Buena Niñez.* Einsiedeln, Switzerland: Bensiger and Co., S.A. 1913.

Vasquez, Jane Atkins and Carolyn Atkins, eds. *Remembering Presbyterian Missions is the Southwest: 25th Anniversary of the Menaul Historical Library.* Albuquerque, New Mexico: Menaul Historical Library, 1998.

Velarde, Pablita. *Old Father Story Teller.* Santa Fé, New Mexico: Clear Light Publishers, 1989.

Williams, Jerry L. *New Mexico in Maps, 2nd Ed.* Albuquerque, New Mexico: University of New Mexico Press, 1986.

INDEX

www.ingramcontent.com/pod-product-compliance
Lightning Source LLC
Chambersburg PA
CBHW031432270326
41930CB00007B/679

* 9 7 8 1 6 3 2 9 3 2 0 9 9 *